Zero-Base Budgeting and
Program Evaluation

Zero-Base Budgeting and Program Evaluation

Joseph S. Wholey
County Board of Arlington, Virginia
The Urban Institute

Lexington Books
D.C. Heath and Company
Lexington, Massachusetts
Toronto

Library of Congress Cataloging in Publication Data

Wholey, Joseph S.
    Zero-base budgeting and program evaluation.

    Includes index.
    1. Zero-base budgeting. 2. Expenditures, Public—Evaluation. I. Title.
HJ2031.W48   350'.722   77-4610
ISBN 0-669-01730-2

Published simultaneously in Canada.

Printed in the United States of America.

International Standard Book Number: 0-669-01730-2

Library of Congress Catalog Card Number: 77-4610

For my wife, Midge

Contents

List of Exhibits

Preface

Zero-Base Budgeting and Program Evaluation shows how simplified zero-base budgeting and program evaluation processes can be used by policymakers to control government costs and achieve policy objectives without creating a massive flow of irrelevant paperwork.

The principal points are established from case studies of zero-base budgeting and program evaluation efforts in local government and in regional and federal agencies. The general conclusion is that the key to efficient, effective government is the personal involvement of top policymakers in setting realistic objectives and then mobilizing needed support. Given the personal commitment of top policymakers to specific objectives, zero-base budgeting and program evaluation provide powerful tools for achieving those objectives.

Acknowledgments

The simplified zero-base budgeting process presented in Chapters 2 and 3 was developed in Arlington, Virginia, and in the Washington Metropolitan Area Transit Authority over the past two years. In Arlington County, particular credit is due County Manager Vernon Ford, Fiscal Analysis Division Chief Anton Gardner, and the department heads, staff, and budget analysts who prepared the zero-base budgeting documents and participated in zero-base budgeting dialogues with County Board members Ellen Bozman, Walter Frankland, Dorothy Grotos, John Purdy, and myself. In the Washington Metropolitan Area Transit Authority, particular credit is due Assistant General Manager/Comptroller William Boleyn and the office and department heads, staff, and budget analysts who prepared the zero-base budgeting documents and participated in zero-base budgeting dialogues with Budget Committee members Cleatus Barnett, Jerry Moore, and myself.

Several of the program evaluation processes presented in Chapter 4 were developed and tested at the Urban Institute over the last several years. Much of the developmental work on these evaluation processes was done by Garth Buchanan, Pamela Horst, Joe Nay, John Scanlon, Richard Schmidt, Alfred Schwartz, John Waller, Donald Weidman, and Thomas White.

John Waller, Joe Nay, John Scanlon, Richard Schmidt, Midge Wholey, and many friends in government provided constructive suggestions as the work progressed. The views presented here are my responsibility and do not represent the position of the Arlington County Board, the Washington Metropolitan Area Transit Authority, the Urban Institute, or other individuals.

Special thanks are due Jane Wholey, Megan Wholey, and Alease Vaughn, who typed the initial and final drafts of the manuscript, often working against incredible odds.

Zero-Base Budgeting and
Program Evaluation

1

Effective Government, At the Lowest Possible Cost

Introduction

In our increasingly urbanized, increasingly complex society, problems multiply— problems that can only be solved by joint public action. Public pressures rise to "do something" about the problems we face. More is expected of government— and government in fact takes on more difficult tasks, attempting to solve problems whose solutions are far from obvious. More government agencies and programs are created, staffed, and funded; but still, government is often weak and ineffective.

Many government programs produce relatively little, especially in compari- son with the money and manpower invested in them. Whether government programs are effective or not, certain truths are evident: Public expectations grow faster than government's ability to meet those expectations; government grows faster than public willingness to tax itself; government programs tend to be inefficient and to lack clear direction; citizens become increasingly alienated when government grows but fails to perform.

In recent years, political rhetoric has changed from promising "more" to promising "efficiency" and "effectiveness":

We must give top priority to a dramatic and thorough revision of the federal bureaucracy, to its budgeting system and to the procedures for analyzing the effectiveness of its many varied services. Tight businesslike management and planning techniques must be instituted and maintained, utilizing the full authority and personal involvement of the President himself. [Jimmy Carter, 1974.] [1]

It is time for us to take a new look at our government, to strip away the secrecy, to expose the pressure of lobbyists, to eliminate waste, to release civil servants from bureaucratic chaos, to provide tough management. . . . As President, I want you to help me evolve an efficient, economical, purposeful, and manage- able government for our nation. I recognize the difficulty, but if I'm elected, it's going to be done! [Jimmy Carter, 1976.] [2]

All of us in this Chamber have heard the American people voice time and again . . . their concern that government is no longer effective nor responsive to their needs. . . . We in Congress have too often satisfied ourselves with the rhetoric of legislation, leaving the hard work of oversight—a fundamental congressional responsibility—to be carried out in a hit-or-miss fashion. . . . Sunset will make us take a closer look at all the component parts [of the Federal budget] . . . to ensure that we are getting the most for the tax dollars we

1

spend.... As part of the review, the authorizing committees [would be] required to explore the potential consequences of cutting into the base of a program's funding rather than simply recommending an incremental funding increase.... [Edmund Muskie, 1977.] [3]

The public wants efficient, effective government. Competing demands for scarce tax dollars mean that more efficient government is an important policy goal. Top policymakers, elected or appointed, arrive in office determined to improve government, find that they can't understand or get control of the programs for which they are responsible, and move on after a year or several years without having made much impact on government efficiency or effectiveness. A new breed arrives, proclaiming that "smaller is better," plays with the form of government processes, but does little or nothing to solve the underlying problems. Government still costs too much in comparison with its accomplishments; government still squanders resources on low-priority, ineffective activities while failing to concentrate its resources on meeting today's public needs.

Government officials often seem to have only two bad choices: either to spend more on government programs and levy far more taxes than we as citizens are willing to pay, or to make arbitrary, uninformed, "meat-axe" cuts in government programs. Efforts to avoid either of these choices tend to produce an even worse alternative, namely, "creative budgeting," in which New York City, the federal government, or some other state or local government borrows millions or billions of dollars to pay for this year's services at the expense of future taxpayers.

Control of large government organizations is complicated and difficult—but is not impossible. This book shows how government can be made more purposeful, manageable, efficient, and effective. In the following pages I show how elected and appointed policymakers can gain control of large government organizations and programs, redirecting government activities to make government more efficient and effective. I show how policymakers can use simplified zero-base budgeting and program evaluation processes to give government clearer direction, save tax dollars, and ensure that citizens receive higher levels of service for the taxes they pay. In comparison with other zero-base budgeting and program evaluation approaches, my approaches minimize paperwork and promote fruitful dialogue among policymakers, agency/program managers, and their budget/evaluation staffs.

This book is directed at policymakers responsible for planning, policy formulation, budgeting, levying taxes, allocating staff, and overseeing the activities and accomplishments of large government organizations. The approaches presented should be of interest to elected and appointed officials and to staff members in both executive and legislative branches of government.

I show how zero-base budgeting and program evaluation can be implemented in ways that efficiently surface important policy issues, bring existing, easily obtainable information to bear on policy decisions, promote fruitful dialogue among policymakers and agency managers, improve policymakers' control over the programs and staff activities for which they are responsible, and promote decisions that improve government services and reduce unnecessary costs.

The Theory of Zero-Base Budgeting and Program Evaluation

Zero-base budgeting (ZBB) reexamines the base of existing program activities, exploring the effects of reducing or reallocating the current levels of resources rather than taking for granted the base of existing programs. Program evaluation identifies the objectives of existing programs and measures program costs and the degree of progress toward program objectives, providing information for policy and management decisions on objectives, resources, and activities.

The typical government policy and management environment is complex (see Exhibit 1-1). As a result of policy debate involving the legislature, the executive, policymakers, agency managers, program managers, and the public, resources are allocated to programs and policies are set. Program management expends program resources, carries out program activities, and produces outputs and impacts that may or may not meet the objectives of the public, of higher-level policymakers, or of program management itself. Resources are usually limited, especially in comparison with public needs and expectations; and time pressures on policymakers are often severe. Feedback on program performance (resources expended, activities undertaken, outputs and impacts achieved) is imperfect. Those at higher policy and management levels often have little information on program performance, even when that information exists or could readily be assembled.

Zero-base budgeting intervenes in the allocation of resources and the setting of government policy; program evaluation, in the provision of systematic information feedback on program performance. Exhibit 1-2 shows how zero-base budgeting and program evaluation are intended to improve government efficiency and effectiveness. In zero-base budgeting (events 1 through 4), operating-level managers reexamine existing program activities, including the effects of reducing programs below current operating levels; examine program alternatives; and set priorities among existing and alternative program activities. Based on operating-level inputs and other information, policymakers then reexamine existing program activities; examine program alternatives; set priorities among existing and alternative program activities; set, maintain, or change policy objectives; and reallocate resources from lower-priority to higher-priority activities. In conjunction with the budget process, policymakers maintain, raise, or lower tax rates (event 5). Given resources and policy objectives, operating-level managers set program objectives (event 6) and manage program activities to

Exhibit 1-1
Government Policy and Management Environment

achieve policy program objectives (event 7). Evaluators assist managers and policymakers by helping them to establish or modify policy/program objectives (events 3 and 6), by evaluating program performance (event 8), and by making this information available to managers and policymakers. In theory, zero-base budgeting and program evaluation thus help policymakers and managers achieve priority objectives (event 9) and control government costs (event 10).

Problems and Concerns

Zero-base budgeting and program evaluation address four problems that face policymakers at all levels of government:

5

Exhibit 1-2
Zero-Base Budgeting/Program-Evaluation Logic

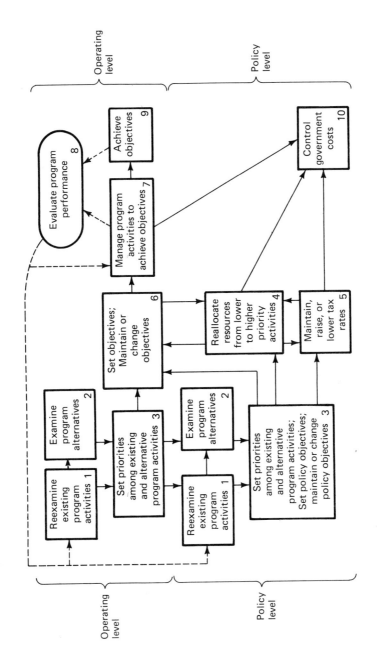

1. Rapid increases in government costs
2. The inertia, inefficiency, and ineffectiveness of many government programs
3. Lack of policy control
4. Inadequate information on program performance

The following pages present solutions to these four problems and address two other concerns about the cost, feasibility, and value of program evaluation:

5. The time and paperwork required
6. The ineffectiveness of past zero-base budgeting and program evaluation efforts

Rapid Increases in Government Costs

Government costs a lot, and government costs are growing. As society becomes more complex, the need and demand for government action increases. Taxes consume a large and growing proportion of society's resources. Government now takes one out of every three dollars we earn in this country, and the trend is up.

Taxpayers see government as a high-cost, inefficient operation. Increasingly, taxpayers complain about taxes and government waste, inefficiency, and mismanagement.

Inertia, Inefficiency, Ineffectiveness

Once initiated, government programs and staff activities tend to go on and on, without serious reexamination of their benefits or priority in relation to possible new programs or to tax-rate reductions.

Government agencies have little incentive to be efficient and are often quite inefficient. Many are neither output oriented nor cost conscious. Every day government programs are created, continued, and expanded in response to pressures from "the special interests" (all of us), with relatively little attention to relationships between costs and results.

In addition, many government programs just don't work very well. Citizen alienation increases; citizen confidence in government declines.

Lack of Policy Control

Government programs and agencies too often lack clear purpose and direction. Policymakers often have little control over the programs and staff activities for which they are responsible. Policymakers find it difficult to affect existing program activities, to reduce the base of existing programs, to redirect existing program activities, or to get agencies and programs moving toward policy objectives.

Even in estimating government costs and revenues, where there is a direct effect on the tax rates that must be levied and on the feasibility of program initiatives within existing tax rates, for example, policymakers tend to operate at the mercy of the bureaucracy. In my own experience and elsewhere, the bureaucracy tends to present budgets that overestimate costs and underestimate revenues, leaving a comfortable surplus after tax rates have been set. At budget time, there appears to be no revenue for policy initiatives. After the budget is adopted and the fiscal year begins, a surplus appears and the bureaucracy is able to undertake activities that might well have been rejected at budget time.[4]

Inadequate Information on Program Performance

At every level of government, policymakers lack systematic information on the performance of existing programs. They have still less information on the likely effects of program alternatives.

Policymakers are unclear on how to set and achieve realistic objectives. It is often not obvious which objectives would be realistic or how objectives might be achieved. In some cases, the public demands results that the government doesn't know how to produce.

Time and Paperwork

Both zero-base budgeting and program evaluation have themselves often represented high-cost, low-payoff processes that did little to save tax dollars or to improve government programs. There is great skepticism that zero-base budgeting can be implemented effectively within the ever-present constraints on the time of government managers, policymakers, and their staffs. Those who know government insist that it doesn't make sense to attempt to review existing operations "from the ground up"—that too much time would be required from program managers and budget analysts to prepare decision packages—and that it would be impossible for top policymakers to effectively review the large number of decision packages for a government of any size. The conventional wisdom is that zero-base budgeting will create a massive flow of paper that will saturate the decision process. There is similar skepticism over the time and money required for systematic evaluation of government program performance.

Ineffectiveness of Zero-Base Budgeting and Program Evaluation

Finally, and most important, experts in political science and public administration believe that, in the end, zero-base budgeting and program evaluation still have little effect on executive-branch or legislative decisions. Since zero-base budgeting and program evaluation are likely to require more effort than government as usual, these experts ask, "Why bother?"

Clearly, the proof is in the pudding: Unless zero-base budgeting and program evaluation have demonstrable effects on policy decisions and produce demonstrable improvements in policymakers' abilities to control government programs and improve government efficiency and effectiveness, there will be little incentive for policymakers, managers, and staffs to invest the necessary time and effort in either process.

Past Experiences and Current Issues with Zero-Base Budgeting and Program Evaluation

Over the past 15 years, many government agencies and private organizations have adopted one or another form of zero-base budgeting or program evaluation, undertaking a reexamination of the costs and results of existing programs and staff activities. A good deal of evidence has accumulated on these efforts.

Zero-Base Budgeting

By now, the story of Peter Pyhrr's use of zero-base budgeting at Texas Instruments and Governor Jimmy Carter's introduction of Pyhrr's zero-base budgeting concepts to Georgia's state government are well known.[5] Though Jimmy Carter and Peter Pyhrr have made impressive claims as to the benefits of zero-base budgeting, other observers have been less enthusiastic.

In 1963 Aaron Wildavsky and Arthur Hammond reviewed a 1962 Department of Agriculture effort to replace incremental budgeting with zero-base budgeting. Wildavsky and Hammond report that Budget Director David Bell had suggested that each program should be "justified from zero" and that Secretary Orville Freeman decided to make his fiscal year 1964 budget a zero-base budget. After interviews with 57 Department of Agriculture policymakers, managers, staff assistants, and budget officers, Wildavsky and Hammond concluded that zero-base budgeting consumed huge amounts of time and energy (at least 180,000 man-hours), produced vast amounts of material justifying agency budget requests, taught new appointees a good deal about Department operations, but produced very little (no more than $200,000 worth) of changes in the Department's budget.[6]

In 1975 George Minmier examined Governor Jimmy Carter's zero-base budgeting efforts in Georgia. After administering questionnaires to the budget analysts who were present during the original implementation of zero-base budgeting, conducting personal interviews with 13 Georgia department heads and with Governor Carter, and examining Georgia's executive budgets for fiscal years 1972, 1973, and 1974, Minmier concluded that zero-base budgeting improved the quality of information available to the governor, to department heads, and to budget analysts; that zero-base budgeting had made an indirect contribution to a reallocation of financial resources (primarily in connection with the reorganization of the state government); but that zero-base budgeting had not made a direct contribution to reallocation of the state's financial resources. After examining the executive budgets for fiscal years 1973, 1974, and 1975 and questioning departmental and staff budget analysts, Minmier found no instances in which budget functions received only the funds requested in the "minimum level of effort" or received less funds than in the previous year's budget. Minmier further noted that the decision package priority rankings were ineffective in adjusting the budget to changes in the level of funds available to the state.[7]

By 1976 the National Association of State Budget Officers and the Congressional Research Service were able to identify at least 11 states that appeared to be using zero-base budgeting, reviewing government program activities from a zero base or from a base below current operating levels.[8]

As promised by Jimmy Carter in his presidential campaign, the federal government is now implementing zero-base budgeting. On February 14, 1977 President Carter fulfilled one of his earliest campaign pledges by issuing an order establishing zero-base budgeting throughout the federal government. President Carter claimed that:

An effective zero-base budgeting system will benefit the Federal Government in several ways. It will:

Focus the budget process on a comprehensive analysis of objectives and needs.

Combine planning and budgeting into a single process.

Cause managers to evaluate in detail the cost-effectiveness of their operations.

Expand management participation in planning and budgeting at all levels of the Federal Government. . . .

By working together under a zero-base budgeting system, we can reduce costs and make the Federal Government more efficient and effective. . . .[9]

The first zero-base budgeting instructions from the Office of Management and Budget provided little indication that zero-base budgeting was to be more than a repackaging of the existing federal budget process, however. Though the Office of Management and Budget required that agencies prepare decision packages on alternative program levels beginning with a minimum level "below which it is not feasible to continue the program, activity or entity because no constructive contribution can be made toward fulfilling its objectives" and that managers rank decision packages in decreasing order of priority (thus achieving the form of zero-base budgeting as it had been practiced in Georgia), the initial zero-base budgeting guidance from the Office of Management and Budget required little that was new in budget preparation, analysis, or justification. The one example included indicated that spending more money would allow creation of more community mental health centers but surfaced no new budget issues either in the federal grant program or in the federal staff support functions for that grant program.[10]

The Office of Management and Budget provided no plausible link between the budget preparation activities it directed and the stated objectives of the new zero-base budgeting system:

... justify the resource requirements for existing activities as well as for new activities ...

... establish, for all managerial levels in an agency, objectives against which accomplishments can be identified and measured ...

... assess alternative methods of accomplishing objectives ...

... analyze the probable effects of different budget amounts or performance levels on the achievement of objectives ...

... provide a credible rationale for the reallocation of resources, especially from old activities to new activities.[11]

In the annual call for budget estimates, the Office of Management and Budget still provided only very general guidance on the implementation of zero-base budgeting, leaving it to the executive agencies to develop the procedures necessary to implement zero-base budgeting. Federal agencies were required to consult the Office of Management and Budget on the decision units to be used in their budget submissions; required to identify minimum funding levels for decision units below current funding levels; allowed to present additional decision packages reflecting higher levels of funding and performance; required to rank the decision packages within each decision unit and within each agency; and allowed to consolidate decision packages to reduce paperwork and review burdens at higher management levels.[12] In response to these requirements, federal agencies implemented zero-base budgeting in a variety of ways.

Though the verdict is not yet in on the effects of zero-base budgeting in the federal government, the following points are fairly clear.

Time and Paperwork Required. Zero-base budgeting takes more of the time of federal managers, policymakers, and staffs than does incremental budgeting. To make the paperwork more manageable and save time at higher management levels, consolidated decision packages are prepared. These consolidated decision packages remove much of the detail and many of the budget choices from the view of higher-level managers and policymakers, however.

Generating Real Policy Choices, Minimizing Game Playing. There is as yet little evidence that the federal government will be more successful than were the earlier efforts of the Department of Agriculture, Texas Instruments, or the state of Georgia in getting managers to propose policy and program alternatives that will allow policymakers to reorder government priorities and improve government efficiency and effectiveness.

Generating Information on the Effects of Policy Choices. By requiring preparation of decision packages representing minimum budget levels below current program levels and requiring agencies to indicate the impact of reduced funding on agency activities and objectives, the federal government's new zero-base budgeting system may begin to provide information on the effects of policy choices. Submission of decision packages representing incremental levels of funding and performance provides the opportunity for lower-level managers and agency heads to present information on the effects of budget choices.

Because of the number of decision packages to be generated, however, the amount of information actually conveyed to policymakers is limited by three conditions: (1) individual decision packages are limited to a maximum of two pages; (2) when decision packages are consolidated, detail is left behind; and (3) the number of decision packages presented limits the opportunity for policymakers to interact with managers to explore the implications of funding alternatives.

Effect on Government. It will take many months to determine the impact of the Carter administration's zero-base budgeting process on executive-branch and congressional decisions and to determine the extent to which there are significant effects on resource allocation, government efficiency, or government effectiveness.

It is clear that the President and the Office of Management and Budget will continue to use zero-base budgeting as *the* federal budget process but will further adapt it in recognition of lessons learned in preparing the fiscal year 1979 budget.

Program Evaluation

Today's interest in efficient government goes far beyond the zero-base budgeting movement. There is widespread interest at all levels of government in evaluating program efficiency and effectiveness. Since the late 1960s, federal spending for program evaluation has expanded manyfold, to more than $200 million per year; and that growth is continuing.[13]

Closely related to, but distinct from, zero-base budgeting is the growing enthusiasm for "Sunset" laws. Under Sunset laws, which exist in several states and have been strongly advocated by Senator Muskie and others in Congress, authority to spend money under government programs exists only for a limited time (say six years), after which either the spending authority is renewed or "the sun sets" on the program, i.e., the program is terminated.

In 1976 Senator Muskie's proposed Government Economy and Spending Act (S.2925) attracted strong support in the Senate but was not reported out of committee. S.2925 would have required that all authorizations of federal programs terminate over a four-year period unless they were reenacted and that all federal programs undergo "zero-base review" (i.e., program evaluation) before they could be reauthorized or reenacted.

In 1977 Senator Muskie and 59 cosponsors reintroduced the proposed Sunset legislation in amended form as S.2, the proposed Sunset Act. As reported out of the Senate Government Affairs Committee, S.2 (now known as the proposed Program Evaluation Act) would:

establish a systematic . . . procedure for reconsideration by Congress of its past program enactments, in order that the Congress can (1) have increased options available to it in the future for allocating Federal resources and establishing Federal policies to meet changing national needs; and (2) exercise greater responsibility for the results of its past legislative work. . . .
The procedure set out in S.2 . . . incorporates two key elements. . . . First, the termination and reauthorization of programs according to a regular [six-year] schedule [the "action-forcing mechanism"] ; and second, the reconsideration of programs of similar purpose at the same time. . . .[14]

Among the findings in the proposed act is that, ". . . in spite of the progress made under budget reform, the Congress has failed to exercise sufficient control over the programs which it has enacted. . . ." Programs would be grouped for reconsideration by budget function, and authorizing committees would be required to assess and report on program accomplishments before recommending reauthorization. Under Title I of the proposed act, all programs that are to be reauthorized would first have to be reconsidered by the authorizing committees with an eye toward answering certain basic questions about the program. "In particular, the committees are required to identify the problems, needs or missions of the program as well as its anticipated accomplishments, to the greatest extent practicable in quantitative and qualitative terms." Under Title III, the Senate and House could select from among those programs a few which they believe ought to receive special attention (intensive evaluation).[15] At this date it is still unclear what, if any, version of the Sunset/Program Evaluation bill will be enacted by the Congress.

Current Issues

As the federal government began to implement zero-base budgeting, there was widespread skepticism that it would achieve President Carter's claims or Office of Management and Budget objectives. Washington had recently seen two other management reforms flower and then wither: the Planning-Programming-Budgeting System (PPB), installed under President Johnson, and Management-by-Objectives (MBO), installed under President Nixon. The Planning-Programming-Budgeting System had been introduced into the federal government by President Johnson in 1965, based on Secretary Robert McNamara's use of the system in the Defense Department. Management-by-Objectives flourished in the federal agencies in the Nixon and Ford administrations after being introduced by Fred Malek and Roy Ash, Deputy Director and Director of the Office of Management and Budget.[16]

Knowledgeable observers have pointed out that the federal government already had a modern budget process; that as Governor Jimmy Carter achieved little real savings in the Georgia budget; zero-base budgeting was likely to generate a flood of additional paperwork; that the necessary information might not be available for zero-base budget analyses; and that politics is likely to carry the day, in any event, after the President's budget is submitted to Congress. For the past two years budget experts have been urging that the federal government "go slow" on zero-base budgeting and Sunset, claiming that the available methods would not permit useful evaluation of government program effectiveness and that zero-base budgeting and Sunset reviews would sink the federal government in a flood of useless paperwork.

Professor Robert Anthony of the Harvard Business School called zero-base budgeting a "fraud," noting that evidence on Georgia's zero-base budgeting experience indicated little if any effect on allocation of resources and concluding that zero-base budgeting offered nothing to the federal government.[17]

On the one hand, many knowledgeable people inside and outside the federal government see zero-base budgeting as the latest fad, predicting that, "ZBB will soon go the way of PPB and MBO." Many special interest groups, on the other hand, fearing that "their" government programs would be adversely affected by close scrutiny, are quick to suggest that, "Not much can be accomplished anyway—so why try?"

Zero-Base Budgeting, Program Evaluation, and Better Government

Contrary to the opinions of budget "experts" and the statements of special interest groups, my experience in goverment convinces me that simplified zero-base budgeting and program evaluation processes are feasible and effective. This book shows how policymakers can use zero-base budgeting and program evaluation to set realistic objectives, evaluate program costs and progress toward priority objectives, and reallocate resources from lower-priority to higher-priority program activities. I show through examples from local and federal government how zero-base budgeting and program evaluation can help policymakers achieve policy objectives and control government costs.

In the county government of Arlington, Virginia, and in the Washington Metropolitan Area Transit Authority, my colleagues and I have developed simplified zero-base budgeting procedures and used simplified zero-base budgeting to improve government efficiency and effectiveness by reducing or eliminating lower-priority programs and staff activities and reallocating resources to higher-priority activities and objectives. Chapters 2 and 3 present case studies of these zero-base budgeting experiences, where high-priority programs were maintained and expanded and millions of dollars in savings to the taxpayers were still achieved. Chapter 5 suggests how zero-base budgeting can usefully be implemented in governments at federal, state, and local levels.

Over the last several years, moreover, my colleagues and I at the Urban Institute have developed and tested program evaluation processes that provide policymakers and managers with timely, relevant information on the promise and performance of government programs. These evaluation processes help policymakers to set clear, realistic, measurable objectives and to obtain valid, reliable information on program performance. Chapters 2, 3, and 4 present examples of timely, useful program evaluation work at local and federal levels; Chapter 6 suggests how program evaluation systems can usefully be implemented.

Long-range planning provides an environment in which zero-base budgeting and program evaluation can contribute a great deal to efficient, effective government. Chapter 7 presents a case study of effective long-range planning.

By examining the likely effects of alternate levels of resources (or alternate ways of accomplishing objectives), zero-base budgeting makes it possible for policymakers to reallocate resources from less-effective, lower-priority activities to higher-priority activities and thus improve the efficiency and effectiveness of government services. Program evaluation provides information needed by policymakers and managers as they establish or modify objectives, allocate resources, and manage program activities.

Zero-base budgeting and program evaluation are significant both for government policymakers and for the citizens and taxpayers they serve. Zero-base budgeting, when implemented with the close involvement of managers who are directly affected and must "live" with the results, works far better than the typical budget process. With the help of subordinates who share the goals of top policymakers, it is possible for government policymakers to review the base of existing programs and achieve substantial cost savings by reducing or eliminating lower-priority activities. Simplified zero-base budgeting saves money, gives policymakers more control over government programs and staff activities, and gives program managers and their staffs the chance to participate in informed priority setting.

As will be shown later, this simplified approach to zero-base budgeting has two advantages over Pyhrr's approach: decision packages are generated only as needed and explicit priority rankings are not required. Paperwork is minimized;

priorities are revealed by budget increases and decreases. Given the personal commitment of top policymakers to specific objectives (e.g., making government more efficient, effective, or economical; reallocating resources from lower-priority activities to higher-priority activities or to tax-rate reductions), zero-base budgeting provides a powerful tool for achieving those objectives.

In addition, zero-base budgeting is feasible with presently available program evaluation techniques. Again, as will be shown later, program evaluation processes are available that quickly produce needed information on program promise and performance. With the close involvement of policymakers who want and will use specific information on program performance, these evaluation processes produce information needed to improve government efficiency and effectiveness.

This book shows how government policymakers can use zero-base budgeting and program evaluation to produce a more efficient, effective, purposeful, and manageable government without overwhelming the decision process with irrelevant information. I present zero-base budgeting and program evaluation processes that have saved millions of dollars and produced documented improvements in government efficiency and effectiveness. With these instruments, policymakers can obtain the information they need to control government activities and government costs, avoiding both the overoptimism of unfulfilled promises and the negativism that gives up on government attempts to solve public problems through joint public action. With this information, policymakers can set realistic objectives, set priorities among programs and staff activities, and either achieve measurable progress toward program objectives or reduce or redirect ineffective programs and staff activities.

Notes

1. Jimmy Carter, announcing his candidacy for President, Washington, D.C., December 12, 1974.

2. Jimmy Carter, accepting the Democratic presidential nomination, New York City, July 15, 1976.

3. Senator Edmund Muskie, introducing the proposed Sunset Act, *Congressional Record* 123, January 10, 1977.

4. See Arnold J. Meltsner and Aaron Wildavsky, *Leave City Budgeting Alone!* (Berkeley: Univ. of California, Oakland Project, 1969), pp. 24-25; Arnold J. Meltsner, *The Politics of City Revenue* (Berkeley: Univ. of California Press, 1971), pp. 118-124; and Jesse Burkhead, *Government Budgeting* (New York: Wiley, 1956), pp. 378-398. Meltsner discusses revenue and expenditure estimating in Oakland, California, in the 1960s; Burkhead goes back as far as the early 19th century.

5. See Peter A. Pyhrr, *Zero-Base Budgeting: A Practical Management Tool for Evaluating Expenses* (New York: Wiley, 1973).

6. Aaron Wildavsky and Arthur Hammond, "Comprehensive Versus Incremental Budgeting in the Department of Agriculture," *Administrative Science Quarterly* 10 (May 1965):321-346. See also Aaron Wildavsky, *Budgeting: A Comparative Theory of Budgeting Process* (Boston: Little, Brown, 1975), pp. 278-294.

7. See George Samuel Minmier, *An Evaluation of the Zero-Base Budgeting System in Governmental Institutions* (Atlanta: Georgia State Univ., 1975); and George S. Minmier and Roger H. Hermanson, "A Look at Zero-Base Budgeting— The Georgia Experience," *Atlanta Economic Review* (July-August 1976):5-12.

8. *Zero-Base Budgeting in the States* (Lexington: The Council of State Governments, September 1976).

9. President Jimmy Carter, "Memorandum for the Heads of Executive Departments and Agencies," Washington, Executive Office of the President, February 14, 1977.

10. Office of Management and Budget, Bulletin No. 77-9, "Zero-Base Budgeting," Washington, Executive Office of the President, April 19, 1977.

11. Ibid.

12. See Office of Management and Budget, Circular No. A-11, "Preparation and Submission of Budget Estimates," Washington, Executive Office of the President, June 1977.

13. See Genevieve J. Knezo, "Program Evaluation: Emerging Issues of Legislative Concern Relating to the Conduct and Use of Evaluation in the Congress and the Executive Branch," Washington, Congressional Research Service, November 1974, p. 1; and Office of Management and Budget, "Resources for Program Evaluation," Washington, Executive Office of the President, 1977. Knezo states that, "federal expenditures for program evaluation are estimated to have risen by more than 500 percent from 1969 to 1974, from $20 million to more than $130 million." The Office of Management and Budget survey indicates that federal program evaluation expenditures totalled $243 in fiscal year 1977: "$169.8 million for contracts and grants, $61.2 million for salaries and benefits, and $12.0 million for other expenses such as travel, supplies, and printing."

14. "Program Evaluation Act of 1977," Washington, Senate Report No. 95-326, Committee on Governmental Affairs, July 1, 1977.

15. Ibid.

16. See Joel Haveman, "Zero-Base Budgeting," *National Journal* (April 2, 1977):183-186.

17. Robert N. Anthony, "Zero-Base Budgeting is a Fraud," *Wall Street Journal* (April 27, 1977).

2

Simplified Zero-Base Budgeting: Theory, Practice, and Results

This chapter examines the theory and purposes of zero-base budgeting, introduces a simplified form of zero-base budgeting through a detailed case study, and shows how this zero-base budgeting process solves several of the major problems faced by government policymakers. The next chapter provides additional case material on this version of zero-base budgeting; a later chapter suggests how the simplified zero-base budgeting process can be implemented at federal, state, and local levels.

Theory and Purposes of Zero-Base Budgeting

In the preceding chapter, the setting in which policymakers typically find themselves at budget time was examined. It was seen that many of the program activities for which policymakers are responsible are costly, inefficient, unmanageable, or of doubtful effectiveness; yet current activities have a momentum that tends to carry them safely through each budget cycle while desirable program expansions or initiatives are sacrificed because of resource constraints. Without detailed knowledge of program activities and objectives, policymakers are unable to identify and reduce lower-priority activities and expenditures and therefore unable to upgrade government efficiency and effectiveness by concentrating resources on higher-priority functions. Given the pressures of other demands on their time, policymakers, unable to penetrate the complexities of program operations, are often reduced to making more or less arbitrary across-the-board percentage increases or reductions—or to making "policy choices" based on little more than the names of programs or agencies.

Policymakers may wish to reduce or eliminate low-priority activities, to save tax dollars, to improve government efficiency and effectiveness, to gain policy control over program activities, to undertake desirable program initiatives within limited resource constraints—but how can they actually do so? How can policymakers learn enough about program activities and results to identify and reduce lower-priority activities, and so restrain the growth of government or gain the resources for higher-priority initiatives? How can policymakers concentrate staff activity, and their own time, on *real* policy alternatives?

What policymakers need is a tool that will clarify what resources are being used to produce what activities with what intended results—and which of these activities might be reduced or eliminated if resources are limited. Policymakers need an efficient way to generate (1) a "shopping list" of feasible budget reductions and budget increases, and (2) information that will illuminate the consequences of these budget choices.

Recognizing that much of the information on existing programs must come from the managers and staffs of those programs, and further recognizing that the interests of policymakers and program staffs may diverge, policymakers need a system that will provide incentives for agency and program managers to review their operations and suggest feasible ways to enhance program efficiency and effectiveness.

Recognizing also that budget "reforms" tend to generate a great deal of paper but few changes in policies or budgets, policymakers need a process that will minimize unnecessary paperwork and focus staff effort on those agency expenditures and staff activities that offer real opportunities for change.

Simplified Zero-Base Budgeting

The key characteristic of zero-base budgeting (as opposed to conventional, or incremental, budgeting) is reexamination and rejustification of the base of existing programs. Zero-base budgeting identifies activities and functions that are of relatively low priority and therefore might be considered for reduction or elimination if resources are needed for other government functions and clarifies the consequences of reducing or eliminating those activities and functions. The fact that a government program or activity was funded last year does not mean that it has to be funded again at the same level, or funded at all. To the extent that reductions are made in the base of existing programs and staff activities, new or expanded programs can then be funded without increasing tax rates.

Our simplified version of zero-base budgeting requires managers of major organizational units to *identify their lowest-priority activities and functions, i.e., those activities which they would give up if they were forced to take (say) a 10 or 15 percent budget reduction.* (At the same time, agency managers are allowed to prepare other "decision packages," proposing possible expansion of existing programs or new program initiatives.) Rather than simply asking the budget staff to project the costs of continuing at current operating levels, policymakers ask agency and program managers to reexamine all their existing program and staff activities, decide which of their present activities are of lowest priority, and identify the consequences of reductions below current operating levels. The resulting decision packages clarify current program and staff activities, agency priorities among those activities, and possible measures of success for the lower-priority activities thus put into question.

By limiting their initial inquiry to budget reductions within the realm of political feasibility (e.g., a range of 10 to 15 percent below current operating levels) and by indicating that resource constraints will require some actual budget reductions, policymakers focus preparation of decision packages on realistic alternatives that in fact merit analysis at policy level. If the first submission is unsatisfactory, policymakers can request additional decision packages showing the effects of further reductions below existing operating levels.

Since agency and program managers are encouraged to provide any evidence they wish on the consequences of making the budget reductions identified in the decision packages, policymakers learn what the program is expected to accomplish if funded at current operating levels.

The second important characteristic of simplified zero-base budgeting is face-to-face dialogue between policymakers and managers of major organizational units. By reducing the volume of decision packages to be prepared and reviewed, simplified zero-base budgeting makes it possible for policymakers, managers, and their staffs to jointly explore the consequences of reducing or eliminating an agency's lowest priority activities; jointly explore the consequences of expanding or initiating higher-priority programs or staff functions; reach agreement on results expected if the program activities in question are continued or expanded; and agree on the least damaging reductions if reductions must be made. In these dialogues policymakers learn what they can expect agencies and programs to accomplish and what data can be obtained to hold them accountable for effective performance.

Therefore, in contrast to other zero-base budgeting approaches, the simplified zero-base budgeting process requires preparation of fewer decision packages, minimizes paperwork, and generates dialogue over real policy alternatives.

How Does the Simplified Zero-Base Budgeting Approach Work in Practice?

My first experience with zero-base budgeting was in preparation of the fiscal 1977 budget for Arlington County, Virginia. Though this first cut at zero-base budgeting generated a good deal of paperwork that has since been eliminated, examination of the Arlington experience should be instructive.

The Setting

Arlington, Virginia, is a 26-square-mile community of approximately 150,000 residents, immediately across the Potomac River from Washington, D.C. An already-developed inner suburb, part of the original District of Columbia, Arlington has in the past 15 years lost population and retail trade while gaining major employment centers and large amounts of high-density office, hotel, and apartment development. Arlington County provides all local government services to its citizens, including those services provided by cities, counties, public school districts, and water-sewer authorities in other parts of the country. Arlington County has an annual operating budget of some $140 million, which finances all local services, including the public schools and a share of the operating costs of the Washington Metropolitan Area Transit Authority. County policy, budget, and tax rates are set by a five-member county board, on which I have served since 1971. Day-to-day operations are in the hands of a county manager, 2200 county employees, a school board appointed by the county board, and 2000 public school employees.

For fiscal year 1977, the county manager proposed a budget that, though essentially a "hold-the-line" budget, was still out of balance by several million dollars. Since a balanced budget is required under the laws of the Commonwealth of Virginia, the manager's proposed budget would have required the board to levy substantially higher taxes. Program initiatives proposed by the county manager and the county board would have further unbalanced the budget and would therefore have required even higher tax rates. The views of county residents, particularly homeowners hard pressed by rising real estate taxes, indicated that a large increase in tax rates was out of the question.

Objective

As a member of the Arlington County Board, I wanted to minimize the need for tax increases while examining county programs to identify (1) those program activities to which the county board would give high priority (maintain or expand) and (2) those program activities which the board would be willing to cut in order to provide revenues for higher-priority county board/staff initiatives. I wanted the board to identify lower-priority, less-essential program activities, avoiding arbitrary, uninformed, "meat-axe" cuts and consequent losses of policy control, political support, and staff morale.

Although the county board had for several years been subjecting the county manager's budget proposals to very close scrutiny, these reviews had usually not succeeded in penetrating very far into the details of agency programs. Facing budget constraints that appeared to be an order of magnitude more difficult than those the county board had faced in other years, the board concluded that a fresh approach was required.

Approach

Some years earlier, I had read Peter Pyhrr's book on zero-base budgeting.[1] Though Pyhrr proposed a budget process that seemed too elaborate for our needs in Arlington, I suggested that the county board use some of the key concepts of zero-base budgeting—in particular, that we get into the base of existing program activities in order to identify possible savings. As a result, the county board adopted a simplified form of zero-base budgeting as a tool for examining and setting priorities among county programs.

To assist our review of the county manager's budget request and the manager's options for program initiatives and expansions beyond those in his recommended budget, the county board requested revised budget submissions from every county agency. We asked each agency for (1) its organization chart; (2) a comparison of authorized staff and existing vacancies; (3) the costs of proposed fiscal year 1977 program activities; and (4) *alternative levels of effort for, or different ways of performing, selected activities that would make possible a 10 percent reduction in its proposed budget.* Each agency was expected to propose reductions from among its lowest-priority activities.

In response, each agency reviewed its existing operations and identified its 10 percent lowest-priority activities in "decision packages" like those in Exhibit 2-1 and Appendix A. In some cases, issue papers or evaluation results were available to supplement the decision packages.

The county board then met with the heads of 25 county departments, divisions, and offices in a series of morning and evening budget work sessions over a two-month period. Both possible program improvements and possible program reductions were examined in these work sessions. Substantive dialogue took place among county board members, department and division heads, and knowledgeable staff over the effects of budget increases or decreases on program performance. Although the dialogues began with the budget changes "proposed" by the county manager and agency heads in the county manager's original budget request and in the zero-base budget submissions, the county board retained the freedom to examine the effects of other budget alternatives.

Results

In these budget work sessions, the county board accepted some of the "proposed" program reductions and program initiatives, in whole or in part, and rejected others. In the end, the board achieved a 5 percent ($2.4 million) net reduction in the county manager's proposed budget for county services, holding the fiscal year 1977 budget for county services below the fiscal year 1976 level (see Exhibit 2-2).

In the simplified zero-base budget process, issues were surfaced and policy choices were made that maintained the services the board considered high priority (e.g., basic county services and add-ons like the police department's successful robbery prevention and take-home patrol car programs), while the board was able to identify and reduce services that it considered relatively low priority (e.g., less-productive police activities, including an ineffective police foot

Exhibit 2-1
Detailed Activity Decision Package: Police Department

No.	Activity Name	Department and/or Division
9001-10	Preventive Patrol	Police

A. Alternative (Different Level of Effort or Different Way of Performance) and Consequences

Alternate Level: 90% of current budget: At the proposed level, which is a reduction in preventive patrol in proportion to the overall departmental 90% estimate, officers would spend 10% less time in random patrol, and would in turn devote some of the savings in time to conducting follow-up investigations for certain categories of cases. Also, the 90% level anticipates a reduction in the amount of time spent on patrol by uniformed officers assigned to "traffic cars" (which are actually back-up cars that supply manpower for crime prevention-type patrol, traffic patrol, accident investigation, and traffic enforcement), and termination of the foot patrol experiment. Some slight increase in crime may result from the reduction; the extent of the increase would be speculative in the absence of a controlled experiment.

Reduction or Addition of Positions (List)

Sworn	Civilian	Total
4.73	0.06	4.79

$ Cost Decrease or Increase

Personnel	Nonpersonnel	Total
$100,666	$15,255	$115,921

	Revenue Impact
	None

B. Alternative (Different Level of Effort or Different Way of Performance) and Consequences

See Detailed Activity Decision Package, page 1 of 29.

Reduction or Addition of Positions (List)

$ Cost Decrease or Increase

Personnel	Nonpersonnel	Total

	Revenue Impact

Source: Arlington County Police Department, Detailed Activity Decision Packages, March 1976

Exhibit 2-2
Arlington, Virginia, Budget for County Services, FY 1977
(Millions of Dollars)

	FY 1976 Actual	1977		
		Requested Budget	Board Adjustments	Approved Budget
County Services	47.5	49.8	−2.4	47.4
+ Contingency/Surplus	0	0.3	+1.0	1.3

patrol program, certain overhead functions, and branch library hours of operation).

Contrary to the typical incremental budget process, in which existing program activities go on without serious scrutiny and budget debate revolves around proposed program initiatives, the size of the overall budget, and the size of the pay raise, the zero-base budget review provided many opportunities for the board to reexamine current operations and reorder priorities. In addition, county board and staff discussions of the decision packages allowed the board to understand existing programs more fully and to make policy choices based on the best evidence available.

In many of its budget actions, the board was able to reach its decision without much information on program performance. In many other instances, however, the board used information on program performance. For example, termination of an unsuccessful police foot patrol program was based on evidence (crime reports, citizen opinion) indicating that the program was ineffective. The addition of local funds to maintain a successful robbery prevention program (after a Law Enforcement Assistance Administration grant expired) was based on evidence that robberies had been reduced below the one-year and five-year averages. The decision to maintain a successful auto tag enforcement program was also based on evidence that the program was effective. Here the board accepted the county manager's conclusions and recommendations relatively easily, since the program would continue to be supported by federal funds rather than by local tax funds. The decision to add funds to the county manager's proposed budget to maintain the successful police take-home patrol car program was more difficult. On a 3-to-2 vote, the board decided to maintain the program after informal evaluation (a geographic plot of reported crimes) indicated that the program was effective.

As part of the budget process, the board also made funds available for new programs initiated by the board and staff; in particular, it made funds available for expanded support for child care programs, transportation improvements, a new tourism development program, and the opening of a juvenile court group home and a geriatric day care center.

Significance

Arlington's fiscal year 1977 budget process showed that a simplified form of zero-based budgeting is feasible and effective. The zero-base budget review surfaced and resolved many real policy issues. Some programs were initiated or expanded even in a time of budget stringency; other programs were reduced or terminated (see Exhibit 2-3).

Substantial changes were made in police department activities, for example. The county board decided to cut preventive patrol, terminating on unsuccessful police foot-patrol experiment; to cut traffic patrol; to reduce investigation of auto accidents involving property damage only;[2] to conduct preliminary investigations of vandalism incidents by telephone; and to make proportionate reductions in police administration. At the same time, the county board also decided to add funds to the county manager's proposed budget to maintain a successful robbery prevention program that had in prior years been funded under a grant from the Law Enforcement Assistance Administration; to maintain a successful police take-home patrol car program the county manager had proposed be eliminated; and to maintain a successful auto tag enforcement program funded through a grant under the Comprehensive Employment and Training Act. Needless to say, it is rare that policymakers penetrate so deeply into police department affairs, especially at budget time.

Substantial budget reductions were also made in department of human resources programs, while increases were budgeted for the same department to open a geriatric day care center and to expand funding for child care and for hospital care of the medically indigent.

Throughout the county government, savings were identified and taken in overhead functions, including planning, personnel, and fiscal analysis.

Very useful dialogue took place between policymakers and top managers as the county board explored the effects of possible increases or reductions in operating levels. Policymakers gained real insight into the implications of policy and budget decisions, since sufficient program performance information was available for most decisions. Information on program performance was available and was used, for example, in the board's decisions to terminate an ineffective police foot patrol experiment; to maintain effective robbery-prevention and police take-home patrol car programs; and to reduce inspections department staff, branch library hours, and institutional foster care services.

The simplified zero-base budgeting process required far less paperwork than would have been required for "traditional" zero-base budgeting. In this budget review, decision packages were prepared only when real decisions were likely. (One problem with a number of the "decision packages" presented in Pyhrr's book was that no policymaker in his right mind would actually choose some of the "alternatives" presented by agency or program managers.)

The simplified zero-base budgeting process did not require a priority ranking of all programs and activities, as advocated by Pyhrr but often found

Exhibit 2-3

Arlington County Budget Decisions (FY 1977): Examples of Issues Surfaced and Policy Choices Made by the County Board

Salary Restraint	−$1,500,000
Police	−$ 720,000
Cut Preventive Patrol (Terminate Unsuccessful Foot Patrol Experiment)	
Cut Traffic Patrol	
Reduce Investigations of Auto Accidents Involving Property Damage Only	
Conduct Preliminary Investigation of Vandalism Incidents by Telephone	
Cut Police Administration	
Police	+$ 329,000
Maintain Successful Robbery Prevention Program (LEAA Grant Expires)	(+$ 248,000)[a]
Maintain Successful Police Take-Home Patrol Car Program	(+$ 41,000)
Maintain Successful Auto Tag Enforcement Program (CETA Grant)	(+$ 19,000)
Inspections	−$ 86,000
Reduce Staff Pending Workload Increase	(−$ 60,000)
Libraries	−$ 114,000
Reduce Branch Library Hours from 60 Hours/Week to 48 Hours/Week	(−$ 77,000)
Commissioner of the Revenue	−$ 40,000
Cut Four Positions	
Human Resources	−$ 365,000
School Health Services	(−$ 43,000)
Volunteer Coordinator	(−$ 12,000)
Institutional Foster Care	(−$ 49,000)
Program Improvements	
Open Juvenile Court Group Home	+$ 31,000
Open Geriatric Day Care Center	+$ 13,000
Expand Funding for Hospital Care of Medically Indigent	+$ 48,000
Establish Contingency Funds for New/Expanded Programs	
Child Care	+$ 100,000
Transportation	+$ 700,000
Tourism Development	+$ 40,000
Lower Overhead	
Land-Use Planning	−$ 74,000
Transportation Planning and Administration	−$ 92,000
Recruitment	−$ 15,000
Tuition Assistance	−$ 55,000
Fiscal Analysis	−$ 35,000

[a]Figures in parentheses are included in Department totals above.

impractical both by Pyhrr and by others. Instead, implicit priorities were revealed as budget choices were made.

Finally, agency managers were closely involved in the budget decisions. Managers understood the budget constraints under which the board was operating, did not play games, committed themselves to specific tasks in return for budgets above 90 percent of the level originally requested, and felt fairly treated by the budget process, even as 100 county staff positions were being eliminated. Many staff initiatives were included in the budget—financed through reductions in lower-priority activities—and the budget changes made by the board were not reversed by the political process (as can easily happen when managers are not sufficiently involved in budget decisions).

In our first experience with this simplified version of zero-base budgeting, the county board achieved the objectives outlined earlier. The county board and county manager were pleased with the results of zero-base budgeting and agreed to use a similar approach in decisions on the fiscal year 1978 budget.

Notes

1. Peter A. Pyhrr, *Zero-Base Budgeting: A Practical Management Tool for Evaluating Expenses* (New York: Wiley, 1973).

2. This decision was reversed more than a year later, when the police department seemed to have *eliminated* investigation of auto accidents involving property damage only.

3 Simplified Zero-Base Budgeting: Will It Work in Other Settings?

The preceding chapter introduced simplified zero-base budgeting in an environment almost perfectly designed to make it appear effective—a time of extreme budget pressure, a fiscally conservative county board unwilling to make substantial changes in tax rates and therefore more than willing to reexamine past program priorities, and a bureaucracy caught unaware as zero-base budgeting was introduced in the midst of the budget decision process.

What would happen if zero-base budgeting became the accepted mode for budget preparation and bureaucrats had more time to "game" the process? What would happen if zero-base budgeting were introduced in a time of program expansion? Though the evidence is still fragmentary, this chapter shows that zero-base budgeting can help policymakers in an expanding, rather than stable, program environment, and can bring about further efficiencies even after the novelty has worn off. Case studies of simplified zero-base budgeting in local and regional governments are presented, how this budget reform is being introduced into a state government is briefly described.

Zero-Base Budgeting in an Expanding Operation

My second experience with simplified zero-base budgeting was in preparation of the fiscal year 1978 budget for the Washington Metropolitan Area Transit Authority, where zero-base budgeting had an even greater impact than in the Arlington experience presented in the preceding chapter.

The Setting

The Washington Metropolitan Area Transit Authority (METRO) operates a fleet of 1900 buses and is constructing a rapid rail/subway system to serve Washington, D.C. and its Maryland and Virginia suburbs. METRO Transit Authority policy is set by a board consisting of six local officials and their alternates; operation of the authority is in the hands of a general manager and 6300 transit authority employees. Though construction of the Metrorail system and purchase of new buses are heavily subsidized by the federal government, transit authority operating costs are paid from the farebox and from taxpayer subsidies, most of which come from the local governments served by the METRO system.

For fiscal year 1978, the METRO general manager proposed an operating budget that included many program improvements; provided for expanded bus and rail operations, including the opening of two new segments of the planned 100-mile subway system; but would have required local governments to provide a $41 million (98 percent) increase in local tax subsidies for Metrobus and Metrorail service. Comments and cries of anguish from local government officials indicated that a 98 percent increase in the METRO operating subsidy would not be tolerated.

Objective

As a member of the METRO Board and the board's three-member budget committee, and as a member of the Arlington County Board, I wanted to cut proposed local tax subsidies for METRO without harming the effectiveness of METRO services to the public.

Approach

My experience in Arlington County seemed directly applicable to METRO's budget problem. I therefore suggested that the METRO budget committee use the concepts and procedures that the county board had used six months earlier in review of Arlington's fiscal year 1977 budget.

Thus the METRO budget committee adopted simplified zero-base budgeting. To assist our review of the general manager's proposed fiscal year 1978 operating budget, the budget committee asked each of the transit authority's 25 operating and staff offices to prepare a revised fiscal year 1978 budget request showing the effects of a 15 percent budget reduction (i.e., a budget 15 percent below the general manager's request) on fiscal year 1978 programs, functions, and services. Each office was expected to propose reductions from among its lowest-priority activities.

In budget committee meetings, the committee communicated a clear message to operating-level managers: "Budget cuts will be made. Those responsible for programs should set priorities." The budget committee indicated that cuts would not be made in an arbitrary manner; instead, those responsible for managing programs and delivering services should set priorities in selecting the activities whose reduction or elimination would be examined in the budget committee's deliberations.

In response, transit authority managers did look seriously at their operations, "proposing" 15 percent reductions from among their lowest-priority activities, in particular, proposing reduction or elimination of many individual programs. The Arlington County fiscal analysis staff made Arlington's zero-base budgeting formats and procedures available to METRO budget analysts; the METRO staff adapted those formats and procedures to the problem at hand. Exhibit 3-1 presents the format in which the resulting decision packages were presented to the budget committee.

In a series of 13 half-day meetings over a three-month period, the budget committee met with the heads and key staff members of each of the authority's 25 operating and staff offices. The committee used the "15 percent reduction exercise" and the general manager's original budget submission as the bases for substantive dialogue with transit authority managers over the effects of possible budget changes (increases or decreases) on the authority's programs, functions, and services to the public. Exhibits 3-2, 3-3, and 3-4 and Appendix B present selected portions of the decision packages considered by the budget committee as well as the budget decisions made by the committee.

Though the dialogue with office heads began with the program/overhead increases and decreases proposed in the original budget submission and in the 15 percent reduction exercise, the budget committee retained the ability to examine the effects of additional alternatives, including either further budget increases or deeper cuts. Based on the original written submission (Exhibit 3-2) and initial dialogue, for example, the office of community services was asked to submit a budget request showing the effects of a 75 percent reduction below the general manager's $581,000 budget request (see Exhibit 3-3).[1] After further dialogue with the office director over the likely effects of each of the items in his "proposed" 75 percent reduction, the budget committee agreed on a 38 percent reduction for community services (see Exhibit 3-4). In other cases, on the basis of the written submissions and the original dialogue, the committee

Exhibit 3-1
Format of Decision Package for Each Transit Authority Operating/Staff Office

Effect of 15 Percent Reduction in FY 1978 Budget Estimates

	FY 1978 Requested	FY 1978 Revised	Percent Change
Positions	_____	_____	_____
Man-Years	_____	_____	_____
Personnel Costs	_____	_____	_____
Nonpersonnel Costs	_____	_____	_____
Total Costs	_____	_____	_____

Effect on FY 1978 Programs, Functions, and Services as a Result of Reductions

[One Paragraph to Many Pages]

Exhibit 3-2

Washington Metropolitan Area Transit Authority Effect of 15 Percent Reduction to FY 1978 Budget Estimates

Office of Community Services

	FY 1978 Estimate	FY 1978 Revised	Change	Percent Change
Number of Positions (year-end)	13	11	(2)	(15)[a]
Number of Man-Years	13	11	(2)	(15)
Personnel Costs	$378,300	$310,994	$(67,356)	(17.8)
Nonpersonnel Costs (List reductions to major items)	$202,700	$182,500	$(20,200)	(10)
Services: Other, $5,200				
Materials and Supplies Consumed: Other,	$ 15,000			
Total Costs	$581,000	$493,444	$(87,556)	(15)

Effect on FY 1978 Programs, Functions, and Service as a Result of Reductions

Reduction of two currently authorized, and filled, positions will impact on the office's ability to provide the current number of official tours. In some cases these would have to be absorbed by other offices. Restrictions on the number of tours by schools and community groups would result. In addition, services provided by Community Services to other offices for audiovisual and photographic support will be severely limited.

"Metro Memo" will be issued 8 times per year instead of 10, as provided in the FY 1978 Budget.

Consumable office materials and supplies have been reduced by $15,000.

Source: Office of Community Services Decision Packages, Washington Metropolitan Area Transit Authority, September 1976.

[a](15) = −15 percent.

concluded that a 15 percent reduction would be excessive and either approved the full budget request or asked office heads to return with a third budget request showing the effects of a 5 percent reduction.

The budget committee also explored opportunities to increase revenue and thereby reduce taxpayer subsidies through increases in fares, expansion of profitable charter service, and increases in advertising revenues.

Results

In its budget review, the budget committee achieved a 10 percent ($20 million) reduction in the proposed METRO operating budget and a 30 percent reduction in proposed local tax subsidies. Operating and staff offices received the resources needed to accomplish agreed-on tasks, and requirements for local tax subsidies increased 40 percent rather than 98 percent. Though operational problems and board policy decisions have affected both costs and ridership and will prevent METRO from realizing the full savings indicated in Exhibit 3-5, local tax subsidies will be substantially lower than the 98 percent increase in the general manager's requested budget.

In the budget process, issues were surfaced and policy choices made that resulted in added transit service, reduction or elimination of lower-priority functions, and no increase in transit authority overhead (see Exhibits 3-5 and 3-6). Under severe budget pressure, the budget committee made conscious decisions to concentrate available resources on operation and maintenance of the expanding Metrorail system. Among the more significant budget changes were reductions in the size of the proposed bus fleet to reflect rerouting of buses to outlying rail stations rather than continuing to run those buses to and from downtown Washington, reduced frequency of revenue collection from Metrorail stations, savings in energy consumption, and reductions in lower-priority overhead and maintenance functions.

The budget committee and the board decided to turn back as many buses as feasible at outlying rail stations, thereby reducing the required number of buses and the operators, mechanics, and operating costs associated with those buses. The projected $5 million savings in Metrobus operating costs were partially offset by the need to increase Metrorail operations at a cost of $500,000. Budget committee decisions on this point were assisted by office of planning and office of budget estimates of the costs of alternative fiscal year 1978 levels of Metrobus and Metrorail service. Budget committee decisions to collect revenues from Metrorail stations every other day rather than daily resulted from a study involving the office of the secretary-treasurer and the office of security.

Based on information presented in each office's decision packages, in face-to-face discussions with office directors, and in issue papers prepared on specific topics, the budget committee achieved substantial savings both in Metrobus and Metrorail operations and in overhead and support functions. It appeared feasible, for example, to save considerable sums by reducing energy consumption in rail operations; by reducing lower-priority community relations, public relations, planning, and marketing activities; by reducing landscape maintenance and cleaning standards for bus shelter and rail stations; and by delaying response time for correcting noncritical problems. In an expanding operation, transit authority overhead/administrative staffing was held to a 0 percent increase over the previous year's budget.

Significance

The METRO Transit Authority experience confirmed the utility of the simplified zero-base budgeting process. The budget committee demanded and got

Exhibit 3-3

Washington Metropolitan Area Transit Authority Effect of 75 Percent Reduction to FY 1978 Budget Estimates

Office of Community Services

	FY 1978 Estimate	FY 1978 Revised	Change	Percent Change
Number of Positions (year-end)	13	4	(9)	(69)
Number of Man-Years	13	4	(9)	(69)
Personnel Costs	$378,300	$ 98,664	$(279,336)	(74)
Nonpersonnel Costs (List reductions to major items)	$202,700	$ 43,950	$(158,750)	(78)
Services: Professional and Technical	35,000	10,470		
Services: Temporary Help	1,700	0		
Services: Contract Maintenance	3,000	0		
Services: Dues and Subscriptions	5,100	0		
Services: Travel and Meetings	4,700	500		
Services: Other	118,000	27,980		
Materials and Supplies Consumed: Other	35,000	5,000		
Leases and Rentals: Equipment	200	0		
Total Nonpersonnel Cost	202,700	43,950		
Total Costs	$581,000	$142,614	$(438,386)	(75)

Effect on FY 1978 Programs, Functions, and Service as a Result of Reductions

Effect on Programs:

1. Loss of Director and Assistant Director. Director provides general policy and order of priorities for office. Conducts liaison with high editorial officials on newspapers and radio and television stations and business and community leaders. Assistant Director provides paperwork support to accomplish tasks of the department. Supervises day-to-day staff activities. Handles personnel matters. Develops budget. Monitors budget to maintain expenditures within limits. Writes Annual Report. Produces official rail and bus maps.
2. The remaining limited staff would necessarily be largely reactive to external demands with little or no time left to generate many things more important to the project.
3. There would be sharply curtailed work with community leaders in civic associations, neighborhoods affected by future METRO construction, the handicapped, businessmen, services, clubs, and the like.
4. There would be no tours for anyone out of this office. Persons referred to WMATA by DOT, Congressmen, and the like would have to be accommodated by persons in other offices, if at all.
5. There would be no school program. Any requests for informational briefings or tours would have to be declined due to lack of manpower.

6. All photography would have to be bought commercially at the inconvenience of finding a *suitable* photographer at a *suitable* price who is available at the *time* the work must be done. This is difficult.

7. The present photograph files would soon become shambles. Retrieval of photos would soon be difficult if not impossible. It would soon become cheaper to hire a photographer, in fact, and reshoot a picture than to find one that is known to be in the files.

8. There would be few photos to be given out to the media. The choice would be thin and soon outdated and fairly useless by virtue of prior publication in other magazines or newspapers.

9. The library would deteriorate equally because of heavy foraging through its contents by scores of students, and with no one to maintain its shelves on a daily basis. Soon citizens would be seeking personal interviews and requiring great blocks of professional time for term papers, classroom assignments, and citizen activity.

10. The secretary and professionals would be unable to help the hundreds of people who drop by this office every year for information, to which they are entitled as taxpayers.

11. This budget would choke the flow of information and lead to an inevitable degeration of the image of METRO and Metrobus, including a loss of public confidence in this project and a willingness to continue supporting it. While today's financial crisis is real, it does *not* reflect a loss of willingness of the people to support public transportation. On the contrary, opinion polls and face-to-face contacts with center-city and suburbanite residents alike show fervent endorsement of the concept and an impatience with the slowness with which construction is proceeding.

Effect on Services:

1. No official bus or rail maps.
2. Only 6 "Metro Memo's" instead of 10 to help get our message out.
3. Minimal or no literature for board or staff to hand out.
4. No Metroclips. Isolation from what's going on, especially how other transit cities are coping with problems we face.
5. Scanty distribution of bus and rail maps, perhaps even sell them.
6. Bare minimum reprints on library shelf (1 or 2).
7. Bare minimum METRO publications on library shelf.
8. Virtually no public distribution of printed information.
9. 100 percent reduction in weekend tour and briefing assistance for Office Director in Phase II.
10. No aerial photography; so no new slides for planners, constructors, environmentalist, and others who use these in their work.
11. 44 percent reduction in COSV photographic effort; continue back-charging other offices.
12. No transcripts of any talk shows or news broadcasts about METRO.
13. No loaning the Office Director to industry meetings to operate the press room.
14. No attendance at APTA conference for any staffer. Not even locally.
15. No motion picture documentation of any station openings and other one-time events.
16. 15 percent reduction in local travel reimbursement (night meetings to civic associations, public hearings, etc.)
17. No consultant help on any board room audiovisual problems.
18. No provision for repairs to board room sound system or motion picture or slide projectors.
19. Minimal maintenance of photo equipment; equipment wears out sooner.
20. Minimal maintenance of mailing lists.
21. No replacement of worn-out dictating system.
22. No replacement of two typewriters.
23. No new photographic equipment for trade-ins of worn equipment. Eventually a degeneration of photographic quality.

Source: Office of Community Services Decision Package, Washington Metropolitan Area Transit Authority, October 1976.

Exhibit 3-4
Board Budget Committee
October 28 and 29, 1976

Decisions

Community Services was reviewed and the following reductions were made:

Eliminated 2 TA-12 Information Specialists	$ 67,500
Eliminated 1 TA-5 Clerk-Typist	13,000
Offset the salary of one TA-10 Photographer with reimbursement for the sale, within and outside the Authority, of his services. If there is not sufficient demand on a pay-as-you-go basis, the position is to be terminated.	23,500
Reduced Professional and Technical by	11,800
Eliminated Temporary Help	1,700
Reduced Contract Maintenance by	1,000
Reduced Dues and Subscriptions by	3,600
Reduced Travel in addition to $3,200 Conference and Meeting reduction by	1,000
Reduced Services—Other by	58,700
Reduced Materials and Supplies—Other by	23,000
Eliminated leases	200
Establish Charge for bus and rail maps	18,200
Total Reduction	$223,200

Planning was reviewed and the following reductions were made:

Eliminated TA-8 Administrative Assistant	$ 16,900
Eliminated TA-8 Transportation Technician	12,600

The Committee agreed to a request to allow a substitution of existing Planning positions for either or both of these positions within existing budgeted funds.

Reduced Professional and Technical as follows:	
Ridership Survey	100,000
Data Processing Services Economic Route Analysis	35,000
Eliminated Temporary Help	10,000
Reduced Printing by a reduction in distribution of public hearing notices	25,000
Total Reduction	$299,500

Source: Board Budget Committee Minutes, Washington Metropolitan Area Transit Authority, October 1976

Exhibit 3-5
The Results: Metro Transit Authority Budget

	FY 1976 Actual	FY 1977 Approved Budget	FY 1978 Requested Budget	FY 1978 Committee Adjustment	FY 1978 Approved Budget
Operating Costs ($ Millions)	128	151	191	−20	171
Positions	5916	6134	7084	−713	6371
Buses	2008	1887	1989	−121	1868
Passengers (Millions)					
Bus-Related	127	125	132	+3	135
Rail-Related	1.5	5.6	54	−1	53
Total Transit	128	129	140	+3	143
Cost/Passenger ($)					
Bus-Related	0.91	0.99	1.03	−.10	0.93
Rail-Related	7.73	4.75	1.02	−.18	0.84
Total Transit	1.00	1.17	1.37	−.18	1.19
Local Subsidy ($ Millions)	38	42	83 (+98%)	−24	59 (+40%)

information describing the effects of possible budget increases and decreases reflecting the priorities of operating and staff offices; budget discussions were more substantive than usual; major policy issues were surfaced and resolved at policy level; operating-level managers were heavily involved in policy decisions; major allocation decisions were made based on already-available program performance information and on information developed through the zero-base review process; "nickel-and-dime" cuts and arbitrary "meat-axe" cuts were avoided; "sacred cows" like security were seriously examined; and paperwork was kept within manageable limits. Through its budget committee, the METRO Board achieved informed policy control of 25 operating and staff offices. Reduction or elimination of lower-priority activities improved transit authority efficiency, freeing resources for higher-priority activities.

The zero-base budgeting process gave transit authority policymaker's far more insight into program operations and staff functions than does the typical budget process.[2] In most instances, informed decisions were feasible with the existing level of information on program performance. Still, many questions

Exhibit 3-6

Metro Transit Authority Fiscal Year 1978 Budget: Examples of Issues Surfaced and Policy Choices Made

Salary Restraint	−$1,300,000
Reroute Many Suburban Buses (Formerly Providing Service to or from Downtown) to Metrorail/Subway Stations outside the Downtown Area	−$4,400,000
Plan for Continued 70-Hour/Week Operations in Fiscal Year 1979	−$1,460,000
Collect Revenue from Rail/Subway Stations Every Other Day Rather than Daily	−$ 376,000
Reduce Energy Consumption in Rail Operations	−$ 866,000
Lower Overhead	
Community Services	−39%
Planning	−15%
Marketing	− 5%
Plant Maintenance	− 9.5%
Reduce Landscape Maintenance and Bus Shelter/Subway Station Cleaning	
Delay Response Time for Correcting Noncritical Problems	

were unanswered at the close of the fiscal year 1978 budget process. In preparation for the fiscal year 1979 budget, 14 follow-up studies were undertaken in such areas as revenue collection alternatives, incentive programs to reduce sick leave, energy conservation, and expansion of charter service.

Finally, the request that all transit authority offices submit their 15 percent lowest-priority activities seemed important in convincing all offices that they were being treated fairly. Policymakers were still free to examine the implications of reductions greater than 15 percent by requesting preparation of additional decision packages on a selective basis.

Based on experience with the fiscal year 1978 METRO budget, both the new general manager and the budget committee decided to use zero-base budgeting in preparing the transit authority's fiscal year 1979 budget.

What Happens the Second Time Around?

My most recent experience with zero-base budgeting was in preparation of Arlington County's fiscal year 1978 budget. Here, zero-base budgeting produced additional savings in a milder budget climate, as agency managers, the county manager and his fiscal analysis staff, and the county board all contributed to improving government efficiency and effectiveness

The Setting

When it was time to prepare our fiscal year 1978 budget, Arlington's financial position had improved considerably. Based on a five-year projection of county costs and revenues, the county board established fiscal year 1978 budget guidelines indicating that county services, the public schools budget, transit authority operating subsidies, and the capital budget all would be increased in fiscal year 1978.

In preparing his fiscal year 1978 budget request, the county manager required that each agency submit possible budget reductions amounting to a 5 percent reduction from the agency's approved fiscal year 1977 budget (see Exhibit 3-7). Each agency was also allowed to propose budget increases above current operating levels.

Based on inputs from county agencies, the public schools, and the fiscal analysis division, the county manager proposed a fiscal year 1978 budget that was approximately in balance (see Exhibit 3-8). In addition, based on the fiscal year 1977 budget process, the county manager decided to present his proposed budget in decision-package format, allowing all county residents and taxpayers the opportunity to support specific budget alternatives. For each county agency, the county manager's recommended budget was presented in terms of major program activities, with staffing and selected performance measures generally reflecting current operating levels (see Exhibit 3-9 and Appendix C). At least 113 decision packages were offered as possible alternatives to the recommended budget; 43 possible increases in county services, totalling approximately

Exhibit 3-7
Arlington, Virginia, Fiscal Year 1978 Budget Guidelines

I. Current Program Levels

No additional positions.

New positions may be added if old positions are eliminated.

II. Reduced Program Levels

Each agency is required to submit—through the preparation of alternative activity levels for selected program activities—the equivalent of a 5 percent budget reduction from the approved FY 1977 budget.

Reductions submitted must be "achievable."

Increased fees may be proposed in lieu of reduced expenditures.

III. Increased Program Levels

Each agency may request the equivalent of a 15 percent increase over the FY 1977 approved budget.

Source: "Fiscal Year 1978 Budget Guidelines," Arlington County Fiscal Analysis Division, August 1977.

Exhibit 3-8
Arlington County Fiscal Year 1978 General Fund

	County Board Guidelines		County Manager Recommended
	Low	High	
County Services	$ 48.8	$ 51.0	$ 50.7
Public Transportation	5.1	5.1	5.1
Debt Service	11.9	11.9	11.7
Public Schools	33.3	35.3	35.7
Community Activities	1.0	1.3	1.3
Contingent	.5	1.0	1.0
Capital	1.0	2.0	1.5
Total Expenditures	$102.0	$108.0	$107.0
Estimated Revenues	$102 to	$108	$107.0[a]

[a]Including $700,000 from a proposed 1 percent tax on restaurant meals. The restaurant meals tax was in fact not authorized by the state legislature and therefore could not be levied.

$900,000; 70 possible reductions in county services, totalling approximately $2,800,000. Not all the decision packages originated in county agencies; the county manager and the fiscal analysis staff proposed a number of decision packages representing possible efficiencies through consolidation of activities cutting across agency lines.

In arriving at his recommended budget, the county manager eliminated 72.5 authorized positions that had not been funded in the fiscal year 1977 budget, deleted several supervisory and support positions, dropped one of 15 trash collection crews, and reduced proposed spending on drug and alcohol treatment programs.

Objectives

As a member of the county board, I wanted to provide for policy changes not included in the county manager's recommended budget, e.g., improvements in existing programs, program initiatives, capital improvements, and (if possible) a modest reduction in the real estate tax rate. I again wanted the board to identify high-priority programs, which would be funded at current or expanded levels, and to identify lower-priority, less-essential services, which would be cut in order to provide resources for higher-priority staff and board initiatives and for a tax-rate reduction.

Approach

Based on the county manager's proposed budget, the decision-package alternatives identified by the county manager, and citizen input on the county manager's recommended budget and on the decision packages, the county board met with the heads of 20 departments, divisions, and offices in a series of morning and evening meetings over a one-month period. Again, substantive dialogue took place among county board members, department/division heads, and knowledgeable staff over the effects of budget increases or decreases on program performance. Although the discussions usually were limited to the decision packages identified by agency heads and the county manager, the board also examined the effects of other budget alternatives.

Results

In the budget work sessions, the county board accepted most of the decision packages "proposing" budget increases and approximately half the decision packages "proposing" budget reductions, initiated several other budget changes not precisely related to any of the decision packages identified by the county manager, and adopted a budget somewhat higher than that which had been recommended by the county manager (see Exhibit 3-10).

Proposals by the county manager, his fiscal analysis staff, and agency heads allowed the board to obtain greater efficiency by consolidating police and fire communications, by dropping one trash collection crew, and by eliminating a number of supervisory and support functions. Without zero-base budgeting it would have been difficult or impossible for the county board to identify these opportunities to save tax money while continuing to provide approximately the same level of services to the public. With the help of staff who knew program operations and were able to set priorities among existing activities, the county board was able to achieve cost savings in low-priority activities that had little if any harmful effect on government operations.

In many instances, the board reallocated funds from lower-priority to higher-priority activities within county agencies. Based on a special study by human resources and fiscal analysis staff, for example, the board decided to maintain a child abuse prevention program that (while federally funded) had proven effective in reducing foster care placements in expensive institutions.

In several instances, the board went beyond the county manager's proposed budget by allocating additional funds to high-priority programs of proven effectiveness, e.g., the State-Local Hospitalization Program, which defrays the hospital expenses of medically indigent residents who are ineligible for Medicare or Medicaid; the Housing Expense Relief Program, which provides local rent-

Exhibit 3-9
Arlington County Decision Package Format (FY 1978 Budget): Police Department

CURRENT ACTIVITY DESCRIPTION — PUBLIC AND EMERGENCY SERVICES

PURPOSE & OBJECTIVES: This activity provides a variety of non-criminal and non-patrol services. This includes licensing (primarily of taxicabs), missing persons investigations, taking care of lost and found property and abandoned automobiles, family crisis intervention, emergency and rescue service, and serving of warrants from other law enforcement agencies.

R E D U C T I O N

ALTERNATIVE 1. DESCRIBE CHANGE, IMPACT AND CONSEQUENCES: This alternative would reduce missing persons investigations. This would mean not investigating a missing persons report unless a person was missing for more than 24 hours or foul play was suspected. Follow-up investigations would be limited to the latter category.

CURRENT ACTIVITY DESCRIPTION — TECHNICAL SERVICES

PURPOSE & OBJECTIVES: The purpose of this activity is to provide technical and support services to the department such as communications and dispatching, record keeping, fingerprinting, photographic services, and data processing.

PERSONNEL (MAN-YEARS) SERVICE CLASSIFICATION	FY 76 ACTUAL	FY 77 BUDGET	FY 78 RECOMM
Sworn:			
Management	2.81	1.63	1.63
Non-management	10.12	10.82	10.82
Civilian:			
Regular	2.65	6.21	6.21
*CETA	0.29	0.52	0.52
Schl. X-ing Grd. Sup. II & I	-0-	-0-	-0-
*Includes 4 Schl. X-ing Grd. I/CETA			
TOTAL	15.87	19.18	19.18
TEMPORARY FUNDS (DOLLARS):	2,915	9,640	9,237

PERSONNEL (MAN-YEARS) SERVICE CLASSIFICATION	FY 78 RECOMM	FY 78 ALT 1	FY 78 CHANGE
Sworn:	2.41	1.69	(0.72)
Civilian:	1.30	0.91	(0.39)
TOTAL	3.71	2.60	(1.11)

PERSONNEL (MAN-YEARS) SERVICE CLASSIFICATION	FY 76 ACTUAL	FY 77 BUDGET	FY 78 RECOMM
Sworn:			
Management	*	0.72	0.72
Non-management	*	19.37	19.37
Civilian:			
Regular	*	29.69	29.69
**CETA	*	4.42	4.42
Schl. x-ing Grd. Sup. II & I	*	-0-	-0-
**Includes 4 Schl. x-ing Grd. I/CETA			
TOTAL		54.20	54.20
TEMPORARY FUNDS (DOLLARS):	6,214	6,277	

FISCAL SUMMARY	FY 76 ACTUAL	FY 77 BUDGET	FY 78 RECOMM
COST			
PERSONNEL	336,142	458,885	400,695
NON-PERSONNEL	48,554	48,106	121,369
TOTAL	384,696	506,991	522,064
REVENUE			
FEES	16,907	21,050	27,490
GRANTS & OTHER	7,341	20,210	23,890
TOTAL	24,248	41,260	51,340
NET GENERAL FUND SUPPORT	360,448	465,731	470,724
% CHANGE FROM FY 77			1
% OF DEPARTMENTAL LOCAL BUDGET			5

FISCAL SUMMARY	FY 78 RECOMM	FY 78 ALT 1	FY 78 (CHANGE +/-)
COST			
PERSONNEL	77,494	61,824	(15,670)
NON-PERSONNEL	23,473	20,567	(2,906)
TOTAL	100,967	82,391	(18,576)
REVENUE			
FEES			
GRANTS & OTHER			
TOTAL			
NET GENERAL FUND SUPPORT	100,967	82,391	(18,576)
% CHANGE FROM FY 78 RECOMMENDED ACTIVITY BUDGET			(19)

FISCAL SUMMARY	FY 76 ACTUAL	FY 77 BUDGET	FY 78 RECOMM
COST			
PERSONNEL	*	1,147,213	990,367
NON-PERSONNEL	*	108,812	48,034
TOTAL	*	1,256,025	1,038,401
REVENUE			
FEES	*	4,200	2,800
GRANTS & OTHER	*	50,121	59,193
TOTAL	*	54,321	61,993
NET GENERAL FUND SUPPORT	*	1,201,704	976,408
% CHANGE FROM FY 76			(19) %
*Included in Program VI			
% OF DEPARTMENTAL LOCAL BUDGET	-0- %	14 %	11 %

PERFORMANCE MEASURES	FY75	FY 76	FIRST HALF OF FY77
Requests for service resulting in police dispatch	67,156	64,672	31,818
Written reports processed	17,725	16,976	8,293
Central record checks conducted	25,733	24,440	9,001
Persons fingerprinted	9,258	10,164	3,706
Criminals identified by crime scene fingerprints	50	50	45

REDUCTION

ALTERNATIVE 1 DESCRIBE CHANGE, IMPACT AND CONSEQUENCES: The Police and Fire Departments maintain separate communications centers on a 24 hours per day, 7 days per week schedule. The basic service functions are
similar, although the daily operations vary greatly in terms of types and volume of calls received
and the staffing patterns. Despite these differences, certain savings can be achieved by integrating
some of the functions, as presented in this alternative.

The Police Department can save over $72,000 by reducing the number of shifts from 5 to 4 (paralleling
the Fire Department's shift pattern). The Fire Department can save approximately $32,000 by training
the civilian personnel currently assigned to the Police Department to be fire dispatchers, thereby
eliminating 4 fire generalist positions (one per shift) by January 1978. In addition, all police and
fire personnel will be trained to handle the other department's calls during peak periods. Some
additional costs (est. $5,000) will be incurred because of equipment modification.

Some initial problems may result from these changes; for example, some efficiency in dispatching calls
will be lost during the initial development and training phase. Also, reducing the police communications unit from 5 to 4 shifts will separate the police officers' shifts from the communications
unit's shifts.

The workload of the Fire Department is projected to increase substantially because of the new emergency
medical service channels currently going into operation. This will make the concurrent phasing in of a
newly trained civilian dispatcher particularly timely.

The benefits of this plan include almost $100,000 savings in personnel costs in FY 1978, along with an
increased ability to handle peak loads through a back up call taking system. This is also a first step
towards building the capability to handle calls through a single emergency number, which may be man-
dated by the state in the near future. The potential long range benefits of such a plan include more
efficient use of existing personnel and more effective service to the public.

CURRENT ACTIVITY DESCRIPTION: INSPECTIONAL SERVICES
PURPOSE & OBJECTIVES: The purposes of inspectional services are to investigate all allegations of police
misconduct and to inspect the police force on a regular basis.

REDUCTION

ALTERNATIVE 1 DESCRIBE CHANGE, IMPACT AND CONSEQUENCES: This alternative would reduce the level of staff
inspections, internal investigations, and strategic intelligence activity currently conducted by
the department. Inspections would be conducted on an as-needed basis only, internal affairs
investigations would be limited in detail and strategic intelligence activity in the community
would be reduced.

PERSONNEL (MAN-YEARS) SERVICE CLASSIFICATION	FY 78 RECOMM	FY 78 ALT 1	FY 78 CHANGE
Police Sergeant	1.0	1.0	-0-
Police Services Technician III	5.0	4.0	(1.0)
* Police Services Technician II	5.0	4.0	(1.0)
Police Service Technician I	20.0	16.0	(4.0)
Communications Clerk/CETA	2.0	2.0	-0-
Police Cadet/CETA	1.0	1.0	-0-
TOTAL	34.0	28.0	(6.0)
TEMPORARY FUNDS (DOLLARS)			

FISCAL SUMMARY	FY 78 RECOMM	FY 78 ALT 1	FY 78 (CHANGE +/-)
COST			
PERSONNEL	524,052	451,792	(72,260)
NON-PERSONNEL	145,412	150,412	5,000
TOTAL	669,464	602,204	(67,260)
REVENUE			
FEES			
GRANTS & OTHER			
TOTAL			
NET GENERAL FUND SUPPORT	669,464	602,204	(67,250)
% CHANGE FROM FY 78 RECOMMENDED ACTIVITY BUDGET			(10) %

PERSONNEL (MAN-YEARS) SERVICE CLASSIFICATION	FY 76 ACTUAL	FY 77 BUDGET	FY 78 RECOMM
Sworn:			
Management	*	2.70	2.70
Non-Management	*	2.23	2.23
Civilian:			
Regular	*	0.12	0.12
*CETA	*	-0-	-0-
School Crossing Guard Supervisor, II & I	*	-0-	-0-
*Includes 4 School Crossing Guard I/CETA			
TOTAL	5.05	5.05	5.05
TEMPORARY FUNDS (DOLLARS)			

FISCAL SUMMARY	FY 76 ACTUAL	FY 77 BUDGET	FY 78 RECOMM
COST			
PERSONNEL	*	76,481	123,110
NON-PERSONNEL	*	9,126	2,860
TOTAL	*	85,602	125,970
REVENUE			
FEES	*		
GRANTS & OTHER	*		
TOTAL	*		
NET GENERAL FUND SUPPORT	* Included in Program VI	* Included in Program VI	
% CHANGE FROM FY 77			47 %

PERSONNEL (MAN-YEARS) SERVICE CLASSIFICATION	FY 78 RECOMM	FY 78 ALT 1	FY 78 CHANGE
Sworn:	4.93	3.97	(.96)
Civilian:	0.12	0.09	(.03)
TOTAL	5.05	4.06	(0.99)
TEMPORARY FUNDS (DOLLARS)			

FISCAL SUMMARY	FY 78 RECOMM	FY 78 ALT 1	FY 78 (CHANGE +/-)
COST			
PERSONNEL	123,110	107,280	(15,830)
NON-PERSONNEL	2,860	2,690	(170)
TOTAL	125,970	109,970	(16,000)
REVENUE			
FEES			
GRANTS & OTHER			
TOTAL			
NET GENERAL FUND SUPPORT	125,970	109,970	(16,000)
% CHANGE FROM FY 78 RECOMMENDED ACTIVITY BUDGET			(13) %

Source: Fiscal Year 1978 Proposed Budget, Volume 1: Activity Decision Packages Arlington, Virginia, February 1977

Exhibit 3-10
The Results: Arlington County Budget, FY 1978
(Millions of Dollars)

| | *FY 1977* | *FY 1978* | | |
| | | *Requested Budget* | *Board Adjustments* | *Approved Budget* |
	Revised			
County Services	$47.8	$50.7	+4.0[a]	$54.7[a]
Public Transportation	1.0	5.1	−1.7	3.4
Debt Service	12.4	11.7	0	11.7
Public Schools	33.1	35.7	−0.5	35.2
Community Activities	1.0	1.3	0	1.3
CETA Transfer: School and Community Activities	0.1	0	+0.3	0.3
Contingency	1.5	1.0	0	1.0
Insurance Reserve	0	0	+0.5	0.5
Capital Improvements	1.7	1.5	+0.6	2.1
Total Expenditures	98.5	107.0	+3.3	110.3
Estimated Revenues	98.5	107.0	+3.3	110.3[b]

[a]Includes an additional $2.1 million in expenditures of CETA (federal funds for job training and public service employment.

[b]Includes a higher-than-expected fiscal year 1977 surplus, higher-than-expected fiscal year 1978 tax collections at existing rates, an additional $2.4 million in CETA (federal) funds for job training and public service employment, and lower revenues resulting from expansion of tax relief for elderly and handicapped people and reduction in the real estate tax rate.

supplement payments to low- and moderate-income residents who are elderly, disabled, or supporting families on low wages; and street and sidewalk repair programs.

The board also provided funds for several policy initiatives, e.g., opening a new recreation center and expanding week-end hours at a countywide recreation center, adding funds for needed capital improvements, establishing a self-insurance program that will more than pay for itself in the first three years, and opening a tourist information center.

Finally, the Board was able to earmark $1,300,000 for tax-rate reduction, expanding tax relief for elderly and handicapped homeowners and reducing the real estate tax rate.

Significance

Arlington's fiscal year 1978 budget process showed that simplified zero-base budgeting is also helpful in a more relaxed budget environment. Again, the zero-base budget review surfaced and resolved many real policy issues. Rather than simply maintaining existing programs and adding new programs, the county manager and the county board reduced or eliminated existing lower-priority activities and achieved efficiencies by eliminating supervisory, support, and overhead positions and by consolidating similar programs in different departments (see Exhibit 3-11).

Very useful dialogue again took place among policymakers, agency managers, and budget staff, as the board explored the effects of possible changes in operating levels. Policymakers maintained informed control over the public programs for which they are responsible. Further, sufficient program performance information was available for most policy and budget decisions. Program performance information was available and was used, for example, in the county board's decision to maintain an effective child abuse prevention program, which reduced the need to place children in expensive institutional foster care settings, and in the county manager's recommendations to streamline several services.

The fiscal year 1978 zero-base budget process required less paperwork than had been required in Arlington's first zero-base budgeting experience. The basic tool was the county manager's 300-page budget proposal, which included the manager's budget message, revenue estimates, organization charts, program ("activity") descriptions, and decision packages for each county department (see Appendix C). Additional issue papers were prepared on selected budget matters. Again, decision packages were prepared only when real decisions were likely; priorities were revealed as budget choices were made; agency managers were closely involved in the budget decisions made by the board; and many staff initiatives were included in the adopted budget.

Action at the State Level

In 1977 the Maryland General Assembly adopted House Joint Resolution No. 119, which requested the Governor to

submit with the FY 1979 budget bill a detailed list from each agency of the programs, positions, and costs which it would elect to cut or increase if its budget were reduced by 10 percent or increased by 5 percent. . . .[3]

Through the new budget procedure, Delegate David L. Scull and the Maryland General Assembly hope to employ Arlington's zero-base budgeting system to solve some of Maryland's financial and budgeting problems.

Maryland adopted our simplified zero-base budgeting approach after investigating alternate budget procedures in Georgia and elsewhere, conducting a demonstration project in "multiple-level budget presentation" with the state highway maintenance division in 1976 and finding that the procedure had "proven to be of value to the General Assembly, and to the agency" and that

44

Exhibit 3-11

Arlington County Budget Decisions (FY 1978): Examples of Issues Surfaced and Policy Choices Made by the County Board

Interdepartmental Efficiencies
Consolidate Police and	–$ 67,000
Fire Communications	– 15,000
Transfer Litter Container	– 51,000
Collection from Utilities to Park Division	+ 31,000

Establish Self-Insurance Program
Annual Savings	– 188,000
Establish Trust Fund (one-time expense)	+ 500,000

Human Resources
Increase Funding for Foster Care of Status	+ 57,000
Offenders (change in State Law)	
Maintain Effective Child Abuse Prevention	+ 18,000
Program (saving some foster care payments)	– 56,000
Maintain and Expand State-Local Hospitalization Program	
Existing program	+ 97,000
Expand eligibility-determination effort	+ 45,000
Increase income eligibility limit	+ 39,000
Eliminate Alcohol Safety Worker	– 21,000
Alcoholic Rehabilitation, Inc.	+ 19,000
Expand Housing Expense Relief Program	+ 66,000

Recreation
Open New Recreation Center	+ 22,000
Special Events	– 20,000
Reduce Hours at Recreation Centers	– 45,000
Open T.J. Center Additional Weekends	+ 11,000
Performing Arts	– 7,000
Temporary Staff	– 10,000

Transportation
Eliminate One Highway Supervisor	– 18,000
Eliminate One Engineering Aide	– 10,000
Expand Street and Sidewalk Repair	+ 250,000
Start-up Automated Traffic Signal Maintenance	+ 30,000

Real Estate Assessment
Eliminate One Record Clerk	– 11,000
Add Senior Appraiser	+ 21,000

Reduce Overhead
3 Planners	– 49,000
Police Court Pay	– 36,000
Courthouse Information Desk	– 10,000
Labor Relations Specialist	– 25,000

Exhibit 3-11 (cont.)

Reduce Overhead *(continued)*	
Contract Night Custodial Services	– $ 30,000
Library Administration	– 15,000
Half-Time Account Clerk	– 5,000
Consumer Protection	
Eliminate Weights and Measures Inspector	– 15,000
Open Tourist Information Center	+ 18,000
Pay Increases	+ 500,000
Convert 16 to 18 Positions from Federally Funded (CETA) to County Funded Positions	+ 165,000
Capital Improvements	+ 600,000
Revenue Reductions	
Expand Tax Relief for Elderly and Handicapped Homeowners	107,000
Reduce Real Estate Tax Rate	1,200,000

... such a procedure has shown it can be the basis for concrete action, both for reductions and increases in expenditures, by a legislative body in Arlington County, Virginia. . . .[4]

The Maryland General Assembly found, in particular, that

the volume of extra paperwork inherent in such a process can be minimized if agencies are not asked to "prioritize" and justify every activity every year, but only to identify a limited increment of lowest and highest priorities, and to justify those specific changes. . . .[5]

Notes

1. Note that the simplified zero-base budget process does in fact justify each agency's budget "from zero." Agency managers review and prioritize all existing activities; policymakers review (say) at least the lowest-priority 15 percent of each agency's activities and as much more as they need to review to justify that agency's budget.

2. In many budget reviews at federal and local levels I have seen budget decisions based primarily on the *names* of the programs.

3. House Joint Resolution No. 119, "Reduction/Increase Budget Format,

Program Evaluation and Coordination with Executive Plans," Annapolis, Maryland General Assembly, 1977 Session.

4. Ibid.

5. Ibid.

4 Evaluating Program Performance

As has been shown, zero-base budgeting provides a decision context in which policymakers become interested in and use program-performance information. Some may object that the program-performance information needed for zero-base budgeting may be available at local level but will not be available at federal or state level. My experience in government convinces me, on the contrary, that concerns about the availability of information for zero-base budgeting and other planning and management processes are unwarranted. In many cases, policy decisions can be made using the program-performance information already available; when specific program performance information is needed but is not already available, that information can often be obtained relatively quickly and inexpensively.

To show that needed program-performance information can be obtained to support zero-base budgeting and other government planning and management processes, this chapter digresses from zero-base budgeting to examine four program-evaluation processes that provide policymakers with needed information on program performance but minimize information costs. These evaluation processes surface key policy and management issues, focus evaluation efforts in areas where evaluation will be worth its cost, and limit data collection and analysis to that which is needed by the policymakers for whom the evaluation is done.

Introduction and Summary

In ordinary language, *program evaluation* is the process of judging the value or worth of government programs. In this sense, zero-base budgeting *is* program evaluation. One of the major concerns about zero-base budgeting, however, is the concern that policymakers will not have sufficient information on program performance to make *good* judgments on the value of government programs.

In this book, we use the term *program evaluation* to mean the systematic measurement of program performance (resource inputs, program activities undertaken, resulting outcomes or impacts), the making of comparisons based on those measurements, and the communication of evaluation findings (measurements and comparisons) for use by policymakers and managers in decisions on government programs. The evaluator may, for example, compare the post-program experience of those served by a program with the preprogram experience of those served, or compare the postprogram experience of those served with some standard of expected accomplishment.[1]

Program evaluation thus supplies what might otherwise be the missing link in zero-base budgeting, providing information on program costs, activities, and results—information that policymakers may need to understand the implications of budget choices. If evaluation identifies programs in which performance is far below policymakers' expectation, policymakers can respond by reducing or eliminating funding or by moving to strengthen the program through reassignment of personnel, addition of resources, or training and technical assistance.

As government programs are undertaken in areas in which the results of government intervention are less obvious, program evaluation is more often considered as a way to obtain information to assist policymakers' decisions on whether to continue, terminate, redirect, or expand the program.

This chapter examines the relationships between zero-base budgeting and systematic program evaluation, reviews problems with past attempts to evaluate the performance of government programs, and presents three quick-feedback program-evaluation processes that provide useful information to busy government policymakers.

Problems Addressed by Program Evaluation

Government programs are often inefficient or ineffective, but government managers are seldom held accountable for efficient, effective performance. Often policymakers and managers lack timely, reliable information on the performance of the programs for which they are responsible. In many programs, even the objectives and measures of success are undefined.

Government too often lacks purpose, lacks clear direction. It is often very difficult to get agreement on clear policy directions (priority objectives to be sought, implementing actions to be taken to achieve those objectives, decisions on who will be held accountable for what, decisions on how progress will be measured), either within large organizations or among organizations. In many public programs, of course, the objective is simply to spend or transfer money or to provide a specified set of services (e.g., support your police department, or put more police officers on patrol). In a good many other cases, however, the program is intended to produce outcomes or impacts beyond the spending of money or the delivery of services (e.g., reduce crime, or improve citizens' sense of security).

In large government organizations and in intergovernmental programs, there typically is a large gap between the policymaker and program reality. Policymakers often have little reliable information on the extent of progress toward policy goals. However, since policymakers are closer to taxpayers and voters than are typical government managers, they will typically be concerned with measures of program costs (costs paid by the taxpayer and costs paid by the user of a government service), measures of citizen/interest-group satisfaction with the services being given, and measures of the impact of the program on those served or on the society in general. Those managing program activities will often be satisfied with measures of service delivered (e.g., frequency of bus service); policymakers will more often concern themselves with the need for services and the costs and impacts of those services (e.g., cost per ride, revenue per ride, taxpayer subsidy per ride, customer satisfaction, and ridership). Evaluation for policymakers will therefore often involve systematic measurements of man-years and dollars expended, systematic measurements of the attitudes and opinions of those served by the program and of other knowledgeable observers, and systematic follow-up surveys to trace the impact of the program on those directly served and on the society.

Evaluators can help policymakers give government clearer direction, hold programs accountable for progress toward specific objectives, and provide information on the effectiveness of program activities in causing observed outcomes or impacts.

Uses of Program Evaluation

Evaluation can be used by an individual policymaker, for example, who uses evaluation information to reach his own conclusions and then persuades others to act. Evaluation can also be used by a group (e.g., an executive management group, a legislative committee, or an appropriations committee) who collectively commission, receive, and use evaluation results in reaching policy decisions on the activities for which they have responsibility.

Over the last several years, in my role as a member of the Arlington County Board, for example, I have used evaluation results to reach policy conclusions for rent supplements and against public housing; against rent control; for legal aid for the poor; for public service employment rather than overemphasis on manpower training; for initiation of a police take-home patrol car program; and for initiation of an experimental manpower program providing income to ex-offenders. In each of these cases, the evaluations came to my attention in my professional work and provided sufficiently conclusive information on program costs and benefits to guide my activities as a board member.

Over the same years, the Arlington County Board (and regional agencies on which I represent Arlington) have used evaluation results in decisions to cancel an unsuccessful police foot patrol program, to maintain successful robbery prevention and police take-home patrol car programs, to cancel a costly paratransit program, to maintain an elderly shopper transportation program, and to reduce and add bus service in response to measured costs and revenues on different bus routes.

Zero-Base Budgeting and Program Evaluation

Zero-base budgeting and program evaluation are complementary tools for achieving policy and management control of government operations. Zero-base budgeting helps policymakers and managers to reach agreement on measurable objectives and realistic performance targets. (Without agreement on objectives and measures of success, program evaluation often resembles a game of blindman's buff or pin-the-tail-on-the-donkey, in which evaluators collect and present information that is almost never sufficiently timely and relevant to influence policy or management decisions.) Conversely, program evaluation provides information on program performance when such information is needed for zero-base budget decisions.

Zero-Base Budgeting and Selection of Evaluation Measures

Selection of valid measures of program performance is not a trivial task.[2] Many of us, for example, are all too familiar with the Vietcong "body counts" that the United States government used for some years to measure the effectiveness of Vietnamese and United States military operations. Reports were inflated as they were passed up the bureaucratic chain; military operations themselves sometimes focused on producing high body counts rather than on more appropriate objectives.[3]

Still some measures of success are needed if policymakers and managers are to maintain contact with reality, detect problems in current program activities, and respond to changing conditions in the environment in which the program operates. Only by periodically reexamining and testing program assumptions can policymakers and managers ensure that program expenditures represent more than income-maintenance programs.

Simplified zero-base budgeting (in particular, the dialogue between policymakers and managers over whether to maintain, reduce, or expand existing programs) tends to bring up to the surface relevant, feasible measures of program performance. The policymaker learns what operational objectives are being sought by program managers; managers learn what policy objectives must be sought to maintain or expand resources; the evaluator learns what program performance data are likely to be desired and what data are likely to be obtainable.

Zero-Base Budgeting and Use of Evaluation Information

Zero-base budgeting increases the likelihood that evaluation information will be used. In my own experience, for example, the Arlington County Board made only sporadic use of evaluation information prior to introduction of zero-base budgeting.[4] We made far more frequent use of program evaluation in the zero-base budgeting environment.

When Arlington adopted zero-base budgeting in the spring of 1976, large numbers of policy choices were forced to the surface; the county board demanded and got information describing the effects of budget changes on program performance; and the board used program-performance information repeatedly in making policy choices that maintained or expanded effective programs while reducing or eliminating lower-priority services and ineffective programs.

In Arlington sufficient program-performance information was available for most zero-base budgeting decisions. The type of information used varied from issue to issue:

Policy Decision	Type Information Used
Cut school health services	Input and process information (cost, subjective impressions on services provided by school nurses)
Reduce branch library hours	Input information (cost, library use by time of day) plus belief that services would not be seriously harmed
Terminate unsuccessful police foot patrol experiment	Formal impact evaluation (crime reports, citizen opinions)
Maintain police take-home patrol car program	Informal impact evaluation (geographic plot of crime patterns)
Maintain successful robbery prevention program	Formal impact evaluation (trends in reported robberies over a six-year period)

The evaluation information did not always come in the decision packages. In some cases, like the decisions over the police foot patrol and robbery prevention programs, policymakers were already aware of the evaluation information; in other cases, like the debate over the police take-home patrol car program, the information was brought to policymakers' attention as a result of dialogue between policymakers and managers over the decision packages. Many decisions did not require outcome or impact information. In certain instances, however, policymakers requested special studies to assist their decisions in the next budget cycle.

Problems with Program Evaluation

The role of program evaluation, then, is to provide information on program performance for use by policymakers and managers in zero-base budgeting and other policy and management decisions. Over the past 15 years, a new industry has been created to evaluate the performance of government programs. The federal government now spends more than $200 million per year for program-evaluation studies, and huge additional sums are spent on program evaluation at state and local levels.

To date, however, relatively little has come from the investments made in evaluation. Most evaluations are not sufficiently timely, relevant, and conclusive to be useful in policymaking or management. Policymakers and managers already get a great deal of informal feedback on program performance without evaluation—through telephone calls, letters, meetings with constituents and interest groups, the press, professional opinion, views from other levels of government, and elections (the ultimate evaluation). This informal feedback is constant, often invalid and unreliable, but still very helpful in keeping policy-makers in contact with program reality. Policymakers have little time and less inclination to read program-evaluation reports, unless they respond directly to the policymakers' own questions and concerns.[5]

Although program evaluation has been a growing area of government activity, there is little evidence that evaluations are being used in policy/management decisions or that government programs are improving as a result. In "Program Management and the Federal Evaluator," my colleagues and I concluded that the ineffectiveness of program evaluation efforts usually results from inadequate definition of the problem addressed by the program, insufficient specification or understanding of the assumed causal links between program inputs/activities and program outcomes/impacts, or lack of management willingness or ability to act on the basis of evaluation information.[6]

In the typical government program, there is no "right" set of performance measures. Government programs often lack clear direction; program objectives are seldom defined in measurable terms. Evaluators are therefore often unclear about what information is needed for what purposes. Evaluators are uncertain about which of the many possible questions about program performance are most important and uncertain about the degree of precision required in answering evaluation questions.

Useful Program-Evaluation Approaches

The keys to effective policy control of large organizations seems to be establishing a small number of clear, realistic, measurable objectives measuring organizational performance in terms of these measures and using the feedback measurements to bring about changes in resources, activities, or objectives. In his books on well-managed private organizations, Peter Drucker shows the feasibility and value of translating vague goals into specific objectives and measurements that allow managers throughout the organization to know what they are intended to accomplish and how they are performing. General Motors, for example, uses *market share* as its key measure of performance; the Bell Telephone System created *customer-satisfaction* standards.[7] Both General Motors and the Bell System used their measures to evaluate organizational performance.

In the public sector, evaluators can do relatively little for policymakers unless policymakers take the time to clarify their priority information needs and the ways in which they intend to use evaluation information. The best vehicle we have found for accomplishing useful evaluation work is a strategy in which policymakers invest in a series of relatively quick and inexpensive evaluation efforts that produce successive increments of information about program promise and performance.

Four program-evaluation processes provide the policymaker with these successive increments of program-performance information: evaluability assessment; rapid-feedback evaluation; outcome monitoring; and intensive evaluation. In the balance of this chapter, I show the contribution that these evaluation processes can make to effective, informed policymaking.

Evaluability Assessment[8]

Evaluability assessment is assessment of the feasibility and likely utility of evaluation in a particular setting. Evaluability assessment clarifies what the program is intended to accomplish (in the eyes of the policymaker for whom the evaluation is to be done) and reveals what measurements of program performance would be feasible and relevant to the information needs of those policymakers. The time scale for evaluability assessment is usually one to four months; the cost, one to six man-months.

The key to useful program evaluation is agreement on relevant, feasible measures of program performance. Research on evaluation reveals that most evaluations are not used because evaluation is undertaken before the program is ready for useful evaluation.[9] In particular, the research shows that evaluation is unlikely to be useful unless certain "evaluation planning standards" are satisfied—(1) program objectives are well defined, (2) causal links between program activities and objectives are plausible and testable, and (3) intended uses of evaluation information are well defined.

1. Program objectives are *well defined* if measures of progress toward objectives have been agreed upon by those who are to use the evaluation information and measurement data are obtainable at reasonable cost and in a reasonable time frame.

2. Causal links are *plausible* if there is evidence that program activities are likely to lead to program objectives.

3. Causal links are *testable* if tests of causal assumptions have been agreed

upon by those who are to use the evaluation information and comparison data are obtainable at reasonable cost and in a reasonable time frame.[10]

4. Intended uses of evaluation information are *well defined* if the intended users of the evaluation information have been identified and the users agree that the evaluation information is needed to assist them in specific decision processes.

Evaluability assessment clarifies the logic of the program (resources, activities, objectives, and causal links between activity and objectives); identifies those portions of the program which are ready for useful evaluation (well-defined objectives; plausible, testable causal links between activities and objectives; well-defined uses for evaluation information); and identifies feasible evaluation and management alternatives.

In evaluability assessment, the evaluator identifies the primary intended users of the planned evaluation; reviews program documentation and interviews program management, agency management, and higher-level policymakers to define intended program activities, objectives, assumed causal links between program activities and objectives, and likely uses of evaluation information; develops a model of the program representing the logic of program activities, objectives, and assumed causal links; reviews field operations to clarify actual program activities, operational objectives, and availability of data; applies the four previously mentioned evaluation planning standards to determine what portion of the program is ready for useful evaluation; and interacts with the intended user to determine which, if any, of the presently available or feasible evaluation alternatives would be sufficiently useful to justify the cost of data collection and analysis. Exhibits 4-1, 4-2, and 4-3 illustrate the products of a hypothetical evaluability assessment.[11]

Exhibit 4-1 presents the logic relating the resource inputs, activities, products, and objectives of a street-cleaning program. The boxes represent events, e.g., allocation of resources (staff, money, and equipment) to street-cleaning, collection of trash, and cleaner streets. The solid arrows represent assumed causal links among resource inputs, program activities, outputs, and objectives.

Exhibit 4-2 presents the results of applying the four evaluation-planning standards to a street-cleaning program. The parentheses indicate the events for which well-defined measures exist. Well-defined measures of program accom-

Exhibit 4-1
Street-Cleaning Program Logic

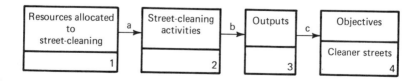

Exhibit 4-2

Street-Cleaning Program: Agreed-On Measures, Comparisons, and Uses of Information

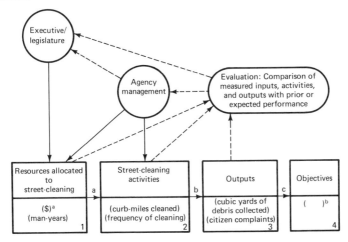

[a]Agreed-on measures are indicated in parentheses.
[b]No measure agreed on.

plishments include dollar expenditures, man-years of effort, curb-miles cleaned, frequency of cleaning various classes of streets, cubic yards of debris collected, and numbers of citizen complaints. Solid arrows indicate the existence of plausible, testable links relating inputs, program activities, and outputs. Dotted arrows represent flows of information, e.g., measurements of program inputs, activities, and outputs; and communication of measures and comparisons to agency management and policy levels. In the absence of agreed-on measures of program objectives, evaluation of program effectiveness is unlikely to be useful to policymakers or program managers.

Exhibit 4-3 presents an evaluation/management alternative to current operations. As discussed later, measurements of street cleanliness/litter could be used in agency management and policy decisions.

Evaluability assessment documents the logic of government programs, those portions of the programs which are ready for useful evaluation, and feasible evaluation/management alternatives to current operations. Presentation of evaluability-assessment results allows the intended user to agree with or correct the program logic, measures of success, and intended uses of evaluation information.

Getting agreement on clear, realistic, measurable objectives is at least half the battle in evaluating the performance of government programs. In many cases, program objectives will be input or process objectives (e.g., spend more money on education of disadvantaged children; establish special tutoring programs). In other cases, program objectives will be outcome or impact objectives (e.g., raise the educational achievement level of children served by the tutoring program; raise the average reading levels in innner-city schools).

Exhibit 4-3
Evaluation/Management Alternative

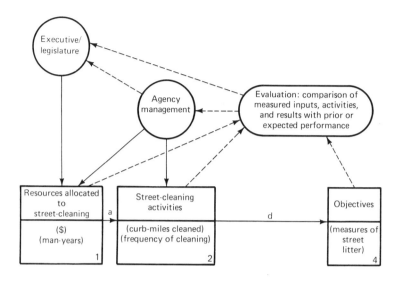

When a program is important enough to warrant policymakers' attention and there is the possibility of special data-collection efforts to meet policymakers' information needs, evaluability assessment can be used to clarify program objectives and measures of success and clarify what additional program-performance information would be sufficiently useful to justify its cost. The time and effort required of evaluators and policymakers, however, mean that evaluability assessment will have to be used selectively.

Rapid-Feedback Evaluation[1][2]

All evaluation information has costs: political costs, bureaucratic costs, costs in time and money. These costs include the costs of agreeing on the measurements and comparisons to be made and agreeing on the anticipated uses of evaluation information; the costs of collecting and analyzing the data; and the costs of reviewing, understanding, and using the resulting information.

In many cases, these costs will be minimal. Some program-performance information will always be available. The types of performance information available and the decision criteria will vary from issue to issue:

Some programs (like general revenue sharing and some other intergovernmental revenue transfers) only have *input objectives.*

Some programs (like social security and public service employment) have *input and process objectives.*

Some programs (like manpower training and drug treatment programs) have *outcome objectives:* intended changes in those directly served by the program.

Some programs (like antismoking, civil rights, and immunization programs) have *impact objectives:* intended changes in the society or the environment.

When a program is being managed to achieve an objective (whether it is an input objective, a process objective, an outcome objective, or an impact objective), performance information will be available on the degree of progress toward that objective. Outcome and impact information will usually be sparse, but many policy decisions do not in fact require outcome or impact information. As Exhibit 4-4 illustrates, many policy decisions can be made using the program-performance information already available.[13] In some cases, additional information will be required to assist executive or legislative decisions.

Rapid-feedback evaluation is a tool for quickly obtaining specific information on program performance, including estimates of program outcome or impact. Rapid-feedback evaluation synthesizes what is already known and what is readily knowable about program performance, in terms of measures and comparisons agreed to by policymakers who require the information for specific decisions. In addition, rapid-feedback evaluation shows what it would cost to improve on this preliminary evaluation by specifying the measures, comparisons, and resources required for more definitive evaluation.

Frequently, all that can be learned from a reasonable expenditure of resources can be learned relatively quickly and inexpensively through rapid-feedback evaluation. The time scale for rapid-feedback evaluation is usually less than six months; the cost, less than two man-years.

Rapid-feedback evaluation is accomplished through a four-step process: collecting readily available information on program performance; estimating the magnitudes of program inputs, activities, outcomes, impacts, and relationships among inputs, activities, outcomes, and impacts; preliminary evaluation; and evaluation design.

Given agreement on a set of performance measures of interest to policymakers (i.e., given the results of evaluability assessment), rapid-feedback evaluation uses program documentation, past evaluation and research studies, expert opinion, quick telephone surveys of program staff or clients, and a limited number of site visits to assemble readily available information on program inputs, activities, outcomes, and impacts. Data collection is limited to the relatively brief period within which evaluation planning and design is being carried out.

Exhibit 4-4

Performance Information Needed versus Performance Information Available

Program	Types of Performance Information[a]				Possible Decisions
	Input	Process	Outcome	Impact	
Antismoking	NNNNN AAAAA	NNNNN AAAAA	NNNNN AAAAA	NNNNN AAAAA	Redesign an ineffective program.
Medicaid	NNNNN AAAAA	NNNNN AAAAA	NNNNN		Redesign programs to achieve outcome objectives. Increase overhead. Establish outcome monitoring system.
Medicare	NNNNN AAAAA	NNNNN AAAAA	NNNNN		
Community Mental Health Centers	NNNNN AAAAA	AAAAA			Maintain, reduce, or expand, depending on resources required for higher-priority programs.
Manpower Training	NNNNN AAAAA	AAAAA	AAAAA		Expand or cut program, depending on unemployment rates.
Safe Streets Act (LEAA Block Grants)	NNNNN AAAAA	NNNNN AAAAA			Cut overhead. Transform into special revenue sharing.
General Revenue Sharing	NNNNN AAAAA				Maintain, reduce, or expand, depending on administration and congressional priorities.

[a]N indicates the types of performance informance likely to be needed or wanted by federal policymakers for decisions they must make to achieve their objectives; A indicates the type of performance information available.

From the available data, the evaluator estimates the ranges of variations of, and functional relationships among, key program variables. In some cases, the evaluator will then have sufficient information to allow a preliminary evaluation of program performance. Often the program is so structured that the evaluator's estimates of program performance could not be greatly improved upon even if a full-scale evaluation were undertaken.

In any case, the evaluator will now have the information needed to allow preparation of designs for one or more feasible evaluations. The evaluator specifies the measurements that would be taken, comparisons that would be made, and the resources required, so that the policymaker has sufficient information for an informed judgment as to whether to proceed with a full-scale evaluation.

For example, in 1973 the Department of Housing and Urban Development asked the Urban Institute to design an evaluation of Operation Breakthrough, a program that was intended to demonstrate the feasibility and value of industrialized housing production.[14] We agreed to design the evaluation through our proposed rapid-feedback evaluation process. We saw rapid-feedback evaluation as a very careful evaluation design process that might develop sufficient data to permit, as a byproduct of evaluation design, a preliminary evaluation of the program.

Operation Breakthrough was initiated at nine prototype sites. Twenty-nine hundred housing units were produced under the demonstration program, and another twenty-three thousand units were built under the Department's Section 236 program. Operation Breakthrough, like many public programs, had a large number of vague goals. There was great diversity among federal officials in their interpretation of Operation Breakthrough goals and in the relative priority they assigned to different goals.

Our rapid-feedback evaluation used available program documentation, existing data, telephone surveys of those involved in or knowledgeable about Operation Breakthrough and housing production, and site visits to four of the nine prototype sites. In the telephone surveys and site visits, 73 people were interviewed.

The rapid-feedback evaluation required approximately 5 months, using 10 man-months of effort. The preliminary evaluation revealed that under Operation Breakthrough housing units were built and marketed as intended; savings and loan institutions did not significantly change their involvement in financing industrialized housing production; Operation Breakthrough did not directly stimulate significant innovation in housing production technology; and there was no evidence that Operation Breakthrough had a measurable effect on the nation's housing production.

The rapid-feedback evaluation of Operation Breakthrough was presented to Congress. With some modifications, the Urban Institute's evaluation design was used for the full-scale evaluation. The two-stage evaluation process provided information more quickly and at lower cost than the single large evaluation originally planned by the Department of Housing and Urban Development.

Many reviewers considered that all that could be learned from evaluation of Operation Breakthrough was learned in the rapid-feedback study. As evaluators we learned, however, that larger samples would have increased users' confidence in the preliminary evaluation.

Outcome Monitoring[15]

If policymakers decide that more information is needed on program results than is already available or is quickly obtainable through rapid-feedback evaluation, two evaluation options are open: *intensive evaluation,* which uses the principles of research design to estimate the causal relationships between program inputs/ activities and the resulting program outcomes and impacts, or *outcome monitoring,* which compares actual program results with prior or expected results but does not attempt to prove whether observed outcomes on impacts were caused by the program. Exhibit 4-5 compares and contrasts these evaluation options with traditional administrative monitoring of program expenditures, services delivered, and numbers served. The next section discusses intensive evaluation; here we examine outcome monitoring.

As defined here, outcome monitoring can be considered to be midway between sophisticated evaluations using experimental and control groups or time series data, on the one hand, and administrative monitoring, on the other. Outcome monitoring may measure the same variables that intensive evaluation would measure; administrative monitoring typically measures input and process only. Intensive evaluation uses control groups, comparison groups, and time-series data in attempting to determine whether program activities cause observed results; outcome monitoring compares actual program results with prior or expected results.

One of the main problems in meeting policymakers' information needs is that in the real world a conclusive evaluation of program effectiveness often is not feasible at all, given the structure of the program, or not feasible at an acceptable cost or within an acceptable time frame. All too often, evaluators are asked to carry out costly, usually inconclusive efforts to address essentially unanswerable questions. The fact that a program was not designed or operated as

Exhibit 4-5

Distinctions among Administrative Monitoring, Outcome Monitoring, and Intensive Evaluation

	Administrative Monitoring	Outcome Monitoring	Intensive Evaluation
Measures Used			
Input	X		X
Process	X		X
Outcome		X	X
Impact		X	X
Measures Compared With			
Expected Results	X	X	
Prior Results	X	X	
Time-Series Data			X
Comparison Groups			X
Control Groups			X

a controlled experiment does not stop policymakers from asking questions that could only be answered with an experiment, but it does mean that the questions may be unanswerable, given the structure of the program and the typical lack of baseline data.

The key to effective outcome monitoring is the establishment of clear, measurable objectives that clarify what the program is trying to accomplish and what information can and will be collected on program performance (e.g., reduce crime as measured by reported robberies and auto thefts; improve citizen satisfaction as measured by telephone surveys of households and neighborhood businesses; or cut red tape as measured by numbers of man-hours required to complete a particular form). If policymakers or managers wish to achieve specific outcomes/impacts and will agree on appropriate measures of success, outcome monitoring can provide timely, reliable reports on the degree of progress toward those outcome/impact objectives.

Outcome monitoring provides specific information on program outcomes/ impacts while the program is still in progress. Measures of success may be quantitative or qualitative. The focus of outcome monitoring is on short-term outcome or impact measures that are related to program goals and can reasonably be expected to be influenced by the program.

Sources of monitoring data may be existing records, newly created project records, special follow-up surveys, or site visits. Data collection may involve a program reporting system in which project managers mail in the data, or may use telephone surveys or site visits to bypass intermediate management levels and deal directly with those in the field or those whom the program is intended to help.

For example, in cooperation with the District of Columbia Department of Environmental Services, the Urban Institute developed a system for monitoring the cleanliness of city streets and alleyways.[16] Monitors observed random samples of streets and alleys, compared litter conditions with those in a set of reference photographs, and assigned numerical ratings ranging from 1 (clean) to 4 (heavily littered). The resulting ratings could then be aggregated to show the cleanliness of the streets and alleys in a geographic area, used to identify problem areas (see Exhibit 4-6), and used to measure the results of regular and special cleanup activities (see Exhibit 4-7).

A number of cities have adopted and used this street-litter monitoring system in the management of sanitation department cleaning of streets, side-walks, and alleyways. Rather than holding the sanitation department and district supervisors accountable for performance defined in terms of process measures, these cities monitor performance in terms of outcomes achieved.

Outcome monitoring moves evaluators away from sterile, academic arguments about standards of proof. In the real world, definitive or conclusive evaluation is often not feasible. Outcome monitoring is usually the least costly, most feasible, and most useful evaluation that can be done under real-world conditions.

Exhibit 4-6

Street Litter Condition Classes and Square Miles in Each[a]

(Map on facing page: Portion of Washington, D.C., area east of Anacostia River)

Litter Condition Class[b]	Square Miles per Class[c]	Percent of Total Area
□ 1.0-1.5[d]	3.80	39
□ 1.6-2.0[d]	3.23	34
□ 2.1-2.5	1.98	21
■ 2.6-3.0	.50	5
■ 3.1-3.5	.10	1
Total	9.61	100

Use of Map: A map of this sort, in conjunction with other information, can be used to estimate manpower requirements for street cleaning operation. For example, assume that city officials decide that the areas of worst conditions (the two most darkly shaded areas, with litter ratings from 2.6 through 3.5) will be upgraded to the ratings of the two best classes (1.0-1.5 and 1.6-2.0). Total area involved is 0.6 square miles, and total curb length of streets (both sides) is found to be 187,000 linear feet. Using productivity data of the D.C. Department of Environmental Services for cleaning streets, sidewalks, and tree box areas, it is calculated that the goal would require *four crew days and two mechanical sweeper days, and an additional two flusher crew work days for flushing gutters.*

Source: Louis H. Blair and Alfred I. Schwartz, *How Clean Is Our City?* (Washington: The Urban Institute, 1972), pp. 54-55. Reprinted with the permission of The Urban Institute.

[a]Size and scale permits display here of only one-third of the actual map devised for this analysis. The data and discussion below them relate to the larger area—all of the District of Columbia east of the Anacosta River.

[b]Condition classes are based on block litter indexes reported April 26-28, 1971. These indexes are the averages of all street inspection ratings for each block. (Alleys not considered in this map and analysis.)

[c]The total area and portions in each class measure all sectors where the District of Columbia government has street cleaning responsibility but exclude sectors under jurisdiction of the National Park Service, Bolling Air Force Base, and so forth. See also note a.

[d]The two cleanest conditions are not differentiated on this map in order to show more clearly the areas that are moderately and heavily littered.

Intensive Evaluation

Intensive evaluation uses the principles of research design to estimate the causal relationships between program inputs/activities and program outcomes/impacts.[17] Because most programs lack suitable control groups, comparison groups, or time-series data, however, most attempts at intensive evaluation fail to produce conclusive information on program performance. When policymakers and program managers agree on the need for intensive evaluation and ensure that the prerequisites exist, intensive evaluations can produce conclusive, compelling information on program effectiveness.

Many texts attempt to show the evaluator how to overcome the prob-

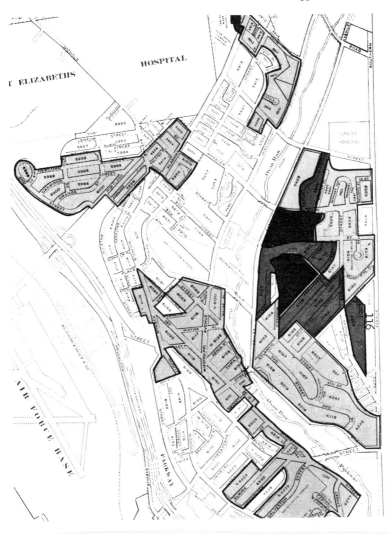

lems of programs that lack experimental and control groups or adequate baseline data.[18] Our approach is different: either policymakers and the evaluator reach agreement that conclusive information is needed on the causal relationships between program inputs/activities and program outcomes and impacts (and then a controlled experiment or quasi-experiment can be considered, using time-series data or experimental and control groups randomly assigned to alternative sets of services) or policymakers and the evaluator reach agreement that less-conclusive information is needed on program effectiveness (in which case they may settle for outcome monitoring based on standards of expected performance). The major point for the policymaker, however, is a clear prior understanding of what will be measured, what

Exhibit 4-7
Illustrative Comparison of Street Litter Ratings

Service Area	Average Sample Litter Rating[a]		Percent of Streets in Sample Rating 2.5 or Worse	
	June 1971	Dec. 1971	June 1971	Dec. 1971
1	2.43	2.11	15	7
2	1.80	1.79	0	0
3	3.13	2.53	61	22
4	2.10	2.32	10	25
5	1.58	1.44	0	0
6	2.71	2.76	31	38
Total[b]	2.38	2.27	29	25

Source: Louis H. Blair and Alfred I. Schwartz, *How Clean Is Our City?* (Washington: The Urban Institute, October 1972), p. 28. Reprinted with the permission of The Urban Institute.

[a]These average ratings would be obtained by inspecting a minimum of 30-50 block-faces in each service area for the low-intensity option and an average of 1000-1500 block-faces in each service area for the high-intensity option. Statistical confidence limits for the averages should also be made available.

[b]Weighted averages based on number of blocks in the respective services areas.

comparisons will be made, and how conclusive will be the resulting information on program performance.

Significance

As suggested previously, program-evaluation work should be focused on specific measurements needed by the policymakers involved in specific decision processes. By providing successive increments of information on the degree to which program objectives have been defined, the extent to which data measuring program performance are available or obtainable, the range of likely costs and effects of program activities, and the extent to which relevant outcome measurements meet or deviate from standards of prior or expected performance, the evaluator can determine the extent to which specific policymakers are willing and able to use evaluation information.

Techniques are available for obtaining timely, useful information on program performance. Useful evaluation work can often be done in the absence of randomly assigned experimental and control groups. The key is agreement between policymaker and evaluator on the evidence (specific measurements and comparisons) needed for policy decisions. Policymakers who want to make government more efficient, effective, purposeful, and manageable can be helped with quick evaluations of program promise and performance, using the evaluability-assessment, rapid-feedback, and outcome-monitoring processes outlined previously.

These program-evaluation processes provide occasions for interaction between the evaluator and the policymakers to whom he provides information. On each occasion, the evaluator provides information on program activities and objectives; policymakers then either focus the evaluator's subsequent efforts in areas where evaluation work will be relevant and useful or terminate evaluation activities when further evaluation effort would be too costly.

These program-evaluation approaches will be helpful in settings in which policymakers wish to direct government programs to achieve outcomes or impacts beyond the delivery of services. These program-evaluation processes provide policymakers with information they need to set realistic objectives and measure progress or lack of progress toward program objectives. The key is policymakers' willingness and ability to set clear objectives and to allocate resources, direct program activities, and maintain or change objectives on the basis of progress or lack of progress toward priority objectives.

In a zero-base budgeting environment, the evaluator has both a better-than-average opportunity to determine policymakers' needs for information and a clearer use for evaluation products. Dialogue among policymakers and managers over decision alternatives provides important clues to relevant measures of program effectiveness; and policy decisions to fund program activities above minimum service levels will often be based on agreement that a specific set of outcomes or impacts is worth achieving (thus providing the basis for subsequent monitoring of program accomplishments). The zero-base budgeting process provides ample opportunity for use of evaluation information: evaluability assessments and rapid-feedback evaluations can assist this year's budget decisions; and outcome monitoring or intensive evaluation can assist in next year's budget decisions.

Notes

1. Evaluation of a manpower program might, for example, measure the costs of training, the types of training, and the postprogram wages of those trained; compare those measurements with preprogram wages of the trainees or with wages of similar individuals not served by the program; and provide the evaluation findings to program administrators and higher-level policymakers.

2. I use the term *measure* in a somewhat more general sense than is usual in program evaluation. Qualitative measures of opinion and expectations are admissible, not simply measures of behavior.

3. See, for example, David Halberstam, *The Best and the Brightest* (New York: Random House, 1972).

4. Evaluations in other communities (which came to my attention in my professional role as program evaluator) helped lay the basis for Arlington's police take-home patrol car program and for programs using paraprofessionals to deliver some police services. Based on a local evaluation of Arlington's Alcohol Safety Action Project, which revealed that the primary benefits would be to those directly served (who would stay out of jail and keep their drivers' licenses), user fees were substantially increased. County board establishment of affirmative action goals and monitoring of county performance in hiring of minorities and women led to the hiring of more blacks and women for Arlington's police force and to the hiring of the first woman firefighter in the United States.

5. As a policymaker, I rarely read evaluation reports that come to me from the outside world. I do not read two-page summaries of evaluation reports; I do not read evaluation reports that come to me with a personal cover note. When evaluation reports come to me from outside groups, I pile them up, unread. When the pile gets too high, I start another pile. Evaluations addressed to a broad audience usually don't communicate with me. If evaluators want to communicate with me, they have to communicate through my staff when a specific decision is to be made, or get their evaluation findings in one of the newspapers I read.

6. Pamela Horst et al., "Program Management and the Federal Evaluator," *Public Administration Review* 34, No. 4 (July/August 1974):300-308.

7. Peter F. Drucker, *Concept of the Corporation* (New York: John Day, 1946; revised edition, 1972); and *Management: Tasks, Responsibilities, Practices* (New York: Harper and Row, 1974).

8. This section is based on Richard E. Schmidt et al., *Serving the Federal Evaluation Market* (Washington: The Urban Institute, 1977); and Joseph S. Wholey et al., "Evaluation: When Is It Really Needed?" *Evaluation* 2, No. 2 (1975):89-93.

9. Horst et al., "Program Management and the Federal Evaluator."

10. As will be seen later, this standard need not be satisfied for useful *outcome monitoring* work, since outcome monitoring does not attempt to prove whether or not program activities cause the observed results.

11. The hypothetical example of evaluability assessment is based on the discussion of street-cleaning programs and systems for evaluating such programs in Louis H. Blair and Alfred I. Schwartz, *How Clean Is Our City?* (Washington: The Urban Institute, 1972).

12. See note 8.

13. I am indebted to John Scanlon of the Urban Institute for this example.

14. This example is based on Donald R. Weidman, Francine L. Tolson, and Joseph S. Wholey, *Summary of Initial Assessment and Evaluation Study Design for Operation Breakthrough* (Washington: The Urban Institute, December 1973; revised, May 1974); and Donald R. Weidman, "An Example of Rapid Feedback Evaluation: The Operation Breakthrough Experience" (Washington: Urban Institute Working Paper, October 1976).

15. This section is based on John D. Waller et al., *Monitoring for Government Agencies* (Washington: The Urban Institute, 1976); Joseph S. Wholey et al., "Evaluation: When Is It Really Needed?"; and Louis H. Blair and Alfred I. Schwartz, *How Clean Is Our City?* (Washington: The Urban Institute, 1972). Further information on outcome monitoring will be found in Harry P. Hatry, Richard E. Winnie, and Donald M. Fisk, *Practical Program Evaluation for State and Local Government Officials* (Washington: The Urban Institute, 1973); Annie Millar, Harry Hatry, and Margo Koss, *Monitoring the Outcomes of Social Services,* Vols. I and II (Washington: The Urban Institute, 1977); and Joseph S. Wholey, *Evaluating Government Performance* (Washington: The Urban Institute, in draft).

16. See Blair and Schwartz, *How Clean Is Our City?*

17. See, for example, Henry W. Riecken and Robert F. Boruch, *Social Experimentation* (San Francisco: Academic Press, 1974).

18. Ibid.

5 Implementing Zero-Base Budgeting

This chapter suggests actions that policymakers can take to enhance the efficiency and effectiveness of zero-base budgeting. I then present a step-by-step outline for implementing zero-base budgeting in a way that will achieve more efficient, more effective grovernment while minimizing problems in this new approach to government planning and management.

Based on the zero-base budgeting experiences previously described, I believe that the strategy outlined here will help policymakers obtain the information and support they need to understand and control agency programs and staff activities, to achieve progress toward policy goals, and to make government more efficient and effective.

Creating the Right Environment

Based on my own experience in government and my study of the experiences of others, I believe that five conditions will greatly improve the efficiency and effectiveness of zero-base budgeting:

1. Personal involvement of top policy officials
2. Executive-branch-legislative-branch negotiations to set broad limits for planning and budgeting
3. Selection of appropriate decision units
4. Creation of incentives for agency managers and their staffs
5. Mobilization of public support

These actions help generate real policy choices and information on the effects of those policy choices, as well as help ensure that zero-base budgeting decisions are implemented in the political and bureaucratic environment.

Personal Involvement of Top Policy Officials

Since zero-base budgeting intervenes in that most political of political processes, the allocation of scarce resources, top policy officials must be involved throughout the budget process. In state or federal government, the governor or President would have to be heavily involved, as Jimmy Carter has been both in

Georgia and in the current federal implementation of zero-base budgeting. At local level, those who must make the final budget choices (the mayor, city manager, or others in positions of power and authority) should be personally involved throughout the budget process. If zero-base budgeting occurs at the initiative of the legislature, the legislative leadership and the entire appropriations committee should be personally involved.

Executive Branch-Legislative Branch Negotiations

When political power is divided between executive and legislative branches, as it is in federal and state governments and in many local governments, each executive-branch decision runs the risk of being reversed when the budget is reviewed, amended, and adopted in the legislature. Politics being the art of the possible, executive-branch officials will be well advised to get legislative-branch concurrence in, or at least understanding of, the context in which zero-base budgeting is to be carried out: broad spending limits, specific priorities for new or expanded programs, areas in which efficiencies and economies will be sought. Such concurrence and understanding will serve policymakers well, helping convince the bureaucracy that spending limits and priorities are real and that zero-base budgeting is more than an exercise.

Selection of Appropriate Decision Units

Selection of appropriate *decision units,* the programs or organizational units for which decision packages will be prepared, is important to adequately inform policymakers of ongoing and proposed activities and objectives without burying policymakers in paper.

If the policymakers doing zero-base budgeting are at the highest level of government (e.g., President, governor, mayor, city manager, legislative leadership, or appropriation committee), the decision units should be agencies, major bureaus or divisions, or budget accounts. In the federal government, for example, the 14 largest budget accounts[1] represent approximately 50 percent of total outlays; the 35 largest budget accounts[2] represent approximately 75 percent of total outlays; the 166 budget accounts above $200 million[3] represent 97 percent of total outlays.[4] In Arlington County and in the METRO Transit Authority, the decision units were 20 to 25 departments, divisions, or operating/staff officers.

If the policymakers doing zero-base budgeting are at agency level, the decision units will be bureaus, operating divisions, and staff offices within the agency. In either case, however, a given set of policymakers should have to deal with no more than 20 to 200 decision units, *not* thousands of decision units.

Creating Incentives for Agency Managers and Staffs

Since effective zero-base budgeting depends on preparation of decision packages that identify lower-priority activities and therefore provide real opportunities for efficiencies and economies that reduce expenditures and staffing below the current level of operations, it is important to motivate agency managers and their staffs to prepare decision packages that in fact offer such opportunities.

In smaller governments, as in Arlington County and in the Washington Metropolitan Area Transit Authority, personal contact between policymakers and key managers may be sufficient to ensure that lower-priority activities are the activities offered up when decision packages are prepared. In larger governments that involve tens of thousands of employees, other incentives may be required to convince agency managers and staffs that changes in existing operations should be seriously examined. Two important incentives would be (1) consideration of program expansions along with program reductions and (2) informal or formal agreement that some portion of budget savings within each agency, bureau, or division would be allocated to the program expansions or initiatives considered highest priority by the management and staff of that agency, bureau, or division.

Mobilizing Public Support

Since zero-base budgeting is likely to threaten some established programs or program activities, all of which are there because somebody wants them, those instituting zero-base budgeting should do all they can to create an environment of public support for the zero-base budget process. Whether the objectives are to avoid tax-rate increases, to reduce tax rates, to justify higher spending, or to reallocate existing resources to fund new programs or improve the efficiency and effectiveness of old programs, each budget choice runs some risk of being reversed by the political process.

If the executive or the leadership of the legislative branch wants to seriously reexamine existing programs, weed out less-important activities, and improve government efficiency and responsiveness, zero-base budgeting offers a golden opportunity to bring the weight of public support to these objectives.

The rhetoric and reality of zero-base budgeting offer good opportunities to mobilize public support for proposed budget. Any policy maker would be proud to report that:

After careful review and reexamination of existing government programs and staffing, we have identified opportunities to save substantial sums, finance high priority services, cut overhead costs, and reallocate staff to improve the efficiency and effectiveness of government programs, reduce tax rates, and still achieve a balanced budget.

Key Events

To illustrate the applications of the simplified zero-base budgeting approach, Exhibit 5-1 indicates how zero-base budgeting could be implemented at the federal level, at state level, or in a large city or county government.

Key events are (1) getting tentative agreement on budget priorities; (2) executive-branch-legislative-branch negotiations; (3) preparation of realistic decision package alternatives; and (4) negotiation and dialogue with those who would be affected by budget choices.

For this presentation, I assume that zero-base budgeting is being implemented in the executive branch. If zero-base budgeting is initiated by the legislative branch, similar negotiations and dialogues should produce similar decisions and "management contracts" leading to more efficient, more effective government.

Getting Tentative Agreement on Budget Priorities

Early in the budget process, the executive (President, governor, mayor, county executive, or city manager) should meet with agency heads and key managers to review existing programs and staff functions and get tentative agreement on executive-branch priorities for the next budget. To meet executive/agency commitments without major tax increases, imposition of a budget ceiling will likely be necessary. Most executive/agency initiatives and program improvements will therefore have to be financed through reallocation of funds or staff from lower-priority activities. To the extent that budget constraints are understood early, budget tradeoffs can be made while there is still time for considered judgments.

Executive-branch agreement on budget priorities and ceilings is helpful because it changes the zero-base budget "exercise" into a team effort to plan together for the most efficient, effective use of the levels of resources likely to be available in the upcoming budget year.

At this point, the executive, agency heads, and key managers should agree on a range of decision alternatives that can reduce the number of decision packages to be considered. At the same time, if the executive agrees to share some portions of agency budget savings by putting those savings into agency initiatives rather than into his personal priorities, he can create incentives for agency identification of real decision alternatives, including both feasible budget reductions and attractive program initiatives/expansions.

Executive-Branch-Legislative-Branch Negotiations

Since the adopted budget will be the product of negotiations between the executive and legislative branches, early contacts between executive-branch

Exhibit 5-1
Key Events in Effective Implementation of Zero-Base Budgeting

January to July 1978: Executive meets with agency heads and key managers to review all existing programs and get tentative agreement on executive budget priorities:[a]

Executive-branch priorities include (say) commitments to specific program initiatives, maintenance of specific high-priority programs, lower tax rates, and a balanced budget.

Lower-priority programs (almost all of them valuable) will have to be reduced or eliminated.

The executive will devote 30 to 40 days to the Fiscal Year 1980 budget/legislative process between March and December 1978.

Effects of reducing program and overhead expenditures by (say) 15 percent will be examined to reveal which expenditures are required to meet executive/agency objectives.[b]

Agencies will set priorities by proposing program initiatives and by offering up (say) the 15 percent lowest-priority expenditures in each program.

Short-term studies will be undertaken where program-performance information would influence executive/legislative decisions.

Executive/agency initiatives will be financed through reallocation from the 15 percent lower-priority functions.

Opportunities for future-year initiatives and savings will be explored as part of the Fiscal Year 1980 budget process.

April to October 1978: Top executive-branch officials meet with legislative-branch leadership and key legislative-branch staff, to explain executive-branch priorities and proposed fiscal constraints—and to get agreement on top program priorities.

April to October 1978: Agency heads and key managers prepare Fiscal Year 1980 decision packages showing the effects of proposed initiatives, including new programs and expansion/redirection of existing programs, and decision packages showing the effects of 15 percent reductions in existing programs and overhead costs.

July to December 1978: Executive meets with agency heads, key managers, and legislative-branch leaders to reach agreement on a realistic budget and legislative proposals reflecting executive/agency/legislative-branch priorities:

Agencies' proposed program, staffing, and overhead initiatives are discussed.

Agencies' proposed 15 percent program, staffing, and overhead reductions are discussed.

When desirable, the effects of reductions of more than 15 percent are explored.

Executive selects reductions in staffing, overhead, and program expenditures from among those offered by the agencies.

Executive selects program, staffing, and overhead initiatives from among those offered by the agencies.

When specific information on program performance is needed for future decisions, agreements are made on how and when the information is to be obtained.

January 1979: Executive submits Fiscal Year 1980 budget and legislative proposals to the legislative branch, documenting changes that will improve government efficiency and effectiveness:

Exhibit 5-1 (continued)

January 1979 (continued)

$X moved from lower-priority to higher-priority programs.

Overhead costs cut by 10 to 15 percent.

Agency staff reallocated to improve efficiency and effectiveness of selected programs.

Measurable increases projected in program performance.

January to May/September 1979: Executive mobilizes public support for budget and legislative proposals.

Results of special studies and short-term evaluation are used in policy debates.

May/September 1979: Legislative branch adopts Fiscal Year 1980 budget and legislation consistent with executive-branch priorities.

---

a*Executive* means President, governor, mayor, county executive, or city manager.

bIn some programs, reduction of lower-priority services to the public will be considered. In other cases, overhead may be reduced, e.g., by combining related programs. When expenditures are relatively uncontrollable in the short run, opportunities for savings over a three-year period will be sought.

and legislative-branch leadership are likely both to allow more realistic executive-branch budget choices and to improve the executive's ability to get major priorities adopted by the legislature.

To the extent that executive and legislature can reach broad agreement on overall budget levels and on priorities for program initiatives and expansions, moreover, the executive can reinforce his agreements with agency heads by communicating whatever degree of executive-branch-legislative-branch understanding exists. The existence of a *real* budget constraint focuses the mind wonderfully on the need to set priorities among existing and proposed programs and on the need to consider reductions in lower-priority programs, services, or overhead functions.

Preparation of Decision Packages

Given a realistic target for overall agency expenditures and a set of executive-branch priorities, agency heads and their key managers would prepare decision packages showing the effects of proposed initiatives, including new programs and expansion or redirection of existing programs, and (say) 15 percent reductions in agency expenditures and staffing. The key here is agency cooperation in actually identifying the *lowest-priority* 15 percent expenditures and staff activities. Both staff/overhead activities and line/service delivery activities should be closely examined.

If high-priority expenditures and activities are identified and offered up as if they were in the low-priority 15 percent, executive-branch policymakers will have to insist on preparation of additional decision packages covering more than 15 percent of an agency's activities.

Once possible reductions are identified, agency managers are free to bring forward any relevant information indicating why the cuts should *not* be made. Here measures of program performance will be identified, and available data will be brought forward to justify continuation of existing activities. Similar information will be presented showing the likely effects of new programs or expansion or redirection of existing programs.

Negotiation/Dialogue

The key to the recommended process is the personal involvement of top executive-branch officials and agency managers in arguing over the decision packages, getting additional information if needed for budget decisions, and reaching agreement on what agency managers will accomplish if reductions are not made or if program expansion/redirection is permitted. Negotiation and dialogue provide the basis for a "management contract" between policymakers and managers—namely, resources are provided for program and staff activities on the understanding that certain results will be achieved. The basis is thus laid for subsequent monitoring of agency performance with respect to the criteria that policymakers and managers thought appropriate for discussion in the budget process.

Implementing Instructions

Exhibits 5-2 and 5-3 outline instructions the executive could use in implementing zero-base budgeting. The Executive's Statement sets the objectives for zero-base budgeting and outlines the process to be followed, focusing attention on priorities for program expansion or tax-rate reduction and on the need to examine both direct services and overhead functions. The Instructions for Submitting Agency Requests require each agency to submit budget requests at current program level and at a level (say) 15 percent below the current program level and permit each agency to submit proposals for new programs or expansion/reduction of existing programs up to (say) 10 percent above current operating levels. The Timetable presents the key decision points in the budget process; and the Budget Format (Exhibit 5-3) requires the agencies to submit their budget requests in a form convenient for subsequent dialogue and decisions.

Exhibit 5-2
Implementing Instructions for Agency Heads

1. *Statement from the Executive*[a]

Administration objectives include (say) increased spending on education, capital improvements, reduced tax rates, and a balanced budget that maintains essential services and minimizes waste.

We will examine each of the appropriations and funds that comprise the budget.

I will focus particular attention on the _____ budget accounts, which are above $_____.[b]

We will also examine programs that cut across budget accounts.

We will look separately at personnel and other overhead functions.

We will involve legislative leaders, and key managers, in our decision on major programs.

Increases in staff and program expenditures will be considered when they can be shown to relate to improvements in program efficiency and effectiveness.

We will also explore the effects of reducing staff and program expenditures by (say) 15 percent.

2. *Instructions for Submitting Fiscal Year 1980 Agency Requests*

Current Program Levels

Each agency is limited to requesting funding for no more than the equivalent number of positions funded in the Fiscal Year 1979 budget.

Costs of current programs will be projected to Fiscal Years 1980, 1981, and 1982, using an inflation factor of _____ percent/year.

Increased Program Levels

Each agency may propose initiatives including new programs or expansion/redirection of existing programs up to 10 percent above current operating levels.

The effects of these initiatives must be described.

If legislation is required for these initiatives, the form of the legislation must be briefly described.

Reduced Program Levels

Each agency is required to submit—through the preparation of alternative funding and staffing levels for each appropriation—the equivalent of a 15 percent reduction from the Fiscal Year 1980 current program level.

The reductions submitted must be "achievable" from both a personnel and program point of view.

The effects of these reductions must be described.

If legislation is required to achieve a 15 percent reduction, the legislative proposal must be briefly described.

3. *Timetable*

Each of you will have two reviews with me to discuss your agency's operations and your recommendations.

Exhibit 5-2 (continued)

3. *Timetable (continued)*

The first review, which will take place before July, will allow us to discuss executive-branch and agency priorities, financial constraints, and the information we will need for executive-branch/legislative decisions on the Fiscal Year 1980 budget and on our legislative proposals.

In the second review, which will take place between July and December, we will discuss the effects of your proposed Fiscal Year 1980 budget/legislative initiatives and the effects of reductions in lower-priority programs and overhead functions.

We will both be in continuing contact with legislative leaders and key legislative staff to explain executive-branch priorities and proposed fiscal constraints—and to get agreement on top program priorities.

To allow us the opportunity for informed dialogue, I am asking you to give me your budget submissions at least 30 days before our meetings.

4. *Budget Format* (See Exhibit 5-3.)

a*Executive* means President, governor, mayor, county executive, or city manager.
bThese budget accounts represent approximately 95 percent of our expenditures.

Notes

1. Old Age and Survivors Insurance, Interest on the Public Debt, Unemployment Trust Fund, Federal Hospital Insurance Trust Fund, Federal Disability Insurance Trust Fund, Civil Service Retirement and Disability Fund, Federal Assistance for Health Care, Operations and Maintenance (Navy), Military Personnel (Army), Public Assistance, Retired Pay (Defense), Federal Financing Bank, Compensation and Pensions, Operations and Maintenance (Air Force).

2. For example, Federal-Aid Highways (Trust Fund), Payments to State and Local Government Fiscal Assistance (General Revenue Sharing), Food Stamp Program.

3. For example, Salaries and Expenses, Department of Housing and Urban Development.

4. See United States Senate, Report 94-1263, *Government Economy and Spending Reform Act of 1976: Report of the Committee on Rules and Administration*, Washington, U.S. Government Printing Office, 1976, Appendix 1, 44-47. Budget accounts are ranked by percentage of total outlays for fiscal year 1977.

Exhibit 5-3
Budget Format

(Sample)

_____ Agency

Effects of 15 Percent Reduction from Current Operating Level

	FY 1977 Actual	FY 1978 Estimated	FY 1979 Estimated	FY 1980 Current Level[a]	FY 1981 Current Level[a]	FY 1982 Current Level[a]	FY 1980 Reduced Level	Percent Change
Positions								
Permanent	1849	1849	1850	1850				
Temporary (FTE)	312	312	300	300				
Man-Years	1976	2098	2100	2100				
Personnel Costs ($ Millions)	36.6	42.9	52.7	56.4	60.3	64.5	47.9	–15
Grants ($ Millions)	588.0	655.2	595.2	636.9	681.5	729.2	541.4	–15
Other ($ Millions)	137.1	164.9	79.6	85.2	91.2	97.6	72.4	–15
Total Obligations ($ Millions)	761.7	863.0	727.5	778.4	832.9	891.2	661.6	–15

Effects on FY 1980-FY 1982 Programs, Functions, and Services as a Result of Reductions

[Describe the Effects in Programmatic Terms]

(Sample)

_____ Agency

Anticipated Effects of Proposed Program Initiatives
(New Programs and Expansion/Redirection of Existing Programs)

	FY 1980	FY 1981	FY 1982
Positions			
Permanent			
Temporary			
Man-Years			
Personnel Costs ($ Millions)			
Grants ($ Millions)			
Other ($ Millions)			
Total Obligations ($ Millions)			

Effects on FY 1980-FY 1982 Programs, Functions, and Services as a Result of Proposed Initiatives

[Describe the Effects in Programmatic Terms. Include Cost Savings in Other Programs]

aAdjusted for Inflation Using Agreed Inflation Factors

Implementing a Program-Evaluation System

Given a set of policymakers who wish to make government more efficient and effective, this chapter presents a strategy for accomplishing useful program-evaluation work.

Evaluation Objectives

The objective of program evaluation is to provide information on program performance that is sufficiently timely, relevant, and conclusive to be useful in policy or management decisions. Policymakers are usually skeptical that useful program evaluation can be accomplished within the time and resources typically available to policymakers, managers, and their staffs. If program evaluation is to be useful, it demands the time of busy people: time to clarify what measures and comparisons are of interest, time to analyze evaluation information, and time to digest and use that evaluation information.

Policymakers are typically unwilling to invest time, money, and staff in an attempt to improve the quality of program-performance information available to them. Already bombarded by more information than they can handle, and with little or no time to absorb additional information, policymakers are often dubious about the value of program evaluation and therefore unwilling to risk much of an investment. Effective implementation of program evaluation must address this concern by minimizing the time and resources required of policymakers and by providing useful information that probably would have been unavailable in the absence of program evaluation.

Timely, Relevant, Conclusive

Most evaluation work has been irrelevant and inconclusive. Research studies of primary interest to researchers, which raise more questions than they answer and generate still other research and evaluation studies but provide no real basis for action, are the rule. Past evaluations usually have not met policymakers' information needs. Effective implementation of program evaluation must therefore identify policymakers' needs for information, determine what types of evidence will be relevant and conclusive, and provide the required evaluation information while policymakers are still interested in the answers.

81

As was shown in Chapter 4, methodologies are now available for identifying relevant questions, determining which questions can be answered and how conclusive those answers would be, and answering the questions that can be answered conclusively within agreed limits on time and resources.

Useful

Unless evaluation provides information that policymakers can use in setting policies and allocating resources, policymakers will have little reason to invest time and other resources in program evaluation. Both to enhance the likelihood that evaluation results will be used and to overcome fears that evaluation will unfairly threaten the existence of the program being evaluated, effective implementation of program evaluation will include prior agreement on both the measures and comparisons to be made and the intended uses of the resulting evaluation information.

Prerequisites for Effective Implementation of Program Evaluation

Based on my experience in government at federal and local levels and my knowledge of others' experiences in federal, state, and local governments,[1] I believe that three actions are necessary for effective implementation of a program-evaluation system:

1. Agreement on clear, realistic objectives and measures of success
2. Identification of likely uses of evaluation information
3. Provision of early and periodic evaluation feedback

Agreement on Clear, Realistic Objectives and Measures of Success

The most important step in establishing a useful program-evaluation system is obtaining policymakers' agreement on the information they need on program costs and results. These decisions on information needs are policy decisions on program objectives: the results to be sought and the results to be minimized or avoided.

Only rarely do policymakers establish clear, realistic, measurable objectives, however. The incentives against setting such objectives are strong. The need to put together a broad coalition in support of a program, to hold that coalition together, and to respond to conflicting pressures tends to produce programs with many vague goals but insufficient resources to achieve much progress in any one direction.[2]

If policymakers wish to establish measurable objectives and hold programs accountable for progress toward those objectives, two steps are necessary:

1. Policymakers agree on the types of objectives for which the program can reasonably be held accountable: input objectives, process objectives, output objectives, or impact objectives.
2. Policymakers agree on relevant measures of success.

A major policy choice is how far out into the environment the policymaker expects the program to have impact. Shall he set objectives on expenditures of resources (more money for education or for health), on delivery of services (provision of remedial reading or health care), on short-term outcomes or impacts (changes in test scores or immunization status), or on longer-term impacts (changes in reading levels or infant mortality rates)? Though the evaluator can help the policymaker by providing information on which measures are obtainable and what evidence there is that the program can influence those measures, the policymaker has to decide which objectives are *his* objectives.

In many cases, policymakers already have sufficient information to set objectives. From prior experience in the program or in related programs or from zero-base budget reviews, policymakers may be able to articulate what inputs, program activities, outputs, or impacts would have to occur to signify accomplishment of program objectives. In other instances, it may be necessary for policymakers and their staffs to explore legislative goals and program reality to gain the information they need to set realistic objectives and measures of success. The evaluability-assessment process described in Chapter 4 can be used, if necessary, in getting agreement on realistic objectives and measures of success.

Identification of Likely Uses of Evaluation Information

To guide the evaluator in decisions on when he must provide information on program performance, how reliable that information must be, and what resources might be invested in evaluation, it is necessary to identify the primary intended uses of the information to be collected. Though policymakers may not be willing to commit themselves fully on the intended uses of evaluation information, some indication of intended use is necessary to clarify what resources should be allocated to program evaluation.

When policymakers are unclear about intended uses of evaluation data, evaluators can produce low-cost preliminary evaluations and monitor the use of those data or the demand for more costly evaluation. The rapid-feedback evaluation and outcome monitoring processes described in Chapter 4 provide such evaluation information at reasonable expenditure levels—and provide the opportunity to test policymakers' use of evaluation information.

Provision of Early and Periodic Evaluation Feedback

Since evaluation is a new and relatively unfamiliar product, it is important for policymakers to get early experience with it. The evaluator measures and makes comparisons based on those measurements; the evaluator provides the resulting information to the policymaker; the policymaker uses or doesn't use the information; the evaluation system then is maintained or modified. Again, the rapid-feedback evaluation and outcome monitoring processes described in Chapter 4 can be used to obtain early and periodic feedback of evaluation information, particularly if the work is done by inhouse staffs or by evaluators who have a continuing relationship with the policymaker. To obtain early and periodic feedback on program performance, policymakers need an evaluation staff that is close enough to them to learn their information needs and has the resources to quickly provide the required data, either from existing data sources, from agency reporting systems or special data-collection efforts, or from directed contractor/consultant efforts.

Key Events

Exhibit 6-1 indicates how program evaluation can be effectively implemented at the federal level, at state level, or in a city or county government. Key events include (1) getting agreement on realistic objectives and relevant measures of success, (2) evaluating program costs and progress toward objectives, (3) making the evaluation information available to policymakers and managers, (4) using the evaluation information to maintain or modify objectives, resources, or program activities, and (5) monitoring the usefulness of evaluation products.

Exhibit 6-1
Key Events in Effective Implementation of a Program-Evaluation System

Step 1   Policymakers agree on realistic objectives and relevant measures of success
Step 2   Evaluating program performance
Step 3   Making evaluation information available to policymakers and managers
Step 4   Using evaluation information to maintain or modify objectives, activities, or resources
Step 5   Monitoring the usefulness of evaluation products

Policymakers Agree on Realistic Objectives

Without agreement on realistic objectives and relevant measures (i.e., at least the *dimensions* along which progress will be measured), evaluators can do little to help policymakers. If policymakers are able to establish realistic, measurable objectives based on their knowledge of policy goals and problem areas, the evaluator can begin his work immediately. The key to the success of Arlington County's Affirmative Action Program, a program designed to encourage the employment and upgrading of minorities, for example, was the establishment of a quarterly monitoring system that reported the numbers and percentages of minorities (in particular, blacks, Spanish-speaking people, and women) in higher-paying and lower-paying jobs in each county agency. Arlington's Affirmative Action Plan for Equal Employment Opportunity required that

... data shall be computed every three months indicating the numbers and percentages of employees in each department by designated pay grade levels from various minority groups such as black and Spanish-American. A similar report shall be prepared on women. ... A summary and evaluation of the above data shall be prepared for distribution to the County Manager, County Board, Civil Service Commission, all department heads and other interested persons.[3]

More typically, policymakers will need more information to help them set measurable objectives. In these instances, the evaluator will have to do some preliminary work (evaluability assessment or rapid-feedback evaluation) to provide policymakers with information on operating-level goals, past program performance, problem areas, and feasible measures of success. In Arlington's Alcohol Safety Action Program, a program for persons arrested for driving while intoxicated, for example, rapid-feedback evaluation was required to clarify possible measures of success and likely program impact on those measures. Based on the rapid feedback, it became clear that the program was unlikely to make a measurable impact on community safety but probably would offer large benefits to those directly served. (Those enrolled would avoid loss of drivers' licenses or jail terms, at a minimum.) In this case an evaluation of program impact on traffic accidents would not have been warranted, because the program had little realistic hope of making measurable impact on such measures.

Evaluating Program Performance

Given a set of realistic objectives and relevant measures of success, the evaluator is ready to provide measures of program performance. For example, in Arlington's Affirmative Action Program, the county personnel department prepared a quarterly report classifying all jobs into two categories (those below and those above a specific grade level) and reporting, for each county agency and each of the two job categories, the number and proportion of minority employees (percent black, percent Spanish-speaking, percent women, etc.).

Making Evaluation Information Available to
Policymakers and Managers

Given prior agreement on the types of program-performance information to be collected and the intended uses of that information, presentation of evaluation information is a relatively simple step. The evaluator reports to policymakers and managers, presenting agreed-upon measures of program cost and performance. In 1976, for example, the Northern Virginia Transportation Commission established the objective that Metrobus riders should pay two-thirds of the cost of Northern Virginia Metrobus service, with local governments (i.e., Northern Virginia taxpayers) paying no more than one-third of the cost of bus service. Each year, the Northern Virginia Transportation Commission receives a report indicating the costs of Metrobus service to Northern Virginia and the proportion of those costs covered by fares paid by Metrobus riders.

Using Evaluation Information

Given prior agreement on the types of program-performance information to be collected and the intended uses of that information, use of the evaluation information is relatively straight-forward. Policymakers and managers use the evaluation information to maintain or modify resources, program activities, or objectives. Quarterly reports on the performance of Arlington's Affirmative Action Program at first produced little action. As the months passed, however, management began to take action to hire and promote minorities and women. Before the federal government's more complicated affirmative action requirements were imposed (saturating the system with a 60-page report that replaced Arlington's one-page quarterly report), Arlington had made important progress toward affirmative action goals, hiring more blacks and women as police officers, for example, and hiring the nation's first woman firefighter.

Monitoring the Usefulness of Evaluation Products

Since evaluation itself represents an overhead cost, policymakers should ensure that the usefulness of evaluation products is monitored and that the monitoring results are used in deciding whether to maintain or modify evaluation activities.

Conclusions

The key to useful evaluation work, therefore, is the first step: the selection of realistic objectives and relevant measures of success. Measures of success may be quantitative or qualitative, based either on observer's impressions or on "hard" evidence. The important thing is to decide what effects the program can reasonably be expected to produce and be held accountable for and how information on program results will be used in policymaking or program management. Depending on the interests of the policymakers, agency managers, or program managers for whom evaluation information is produced, evaluation measures may include measures of citizen/interest-group satisfaction, follow-up surveys of those served by the program, or measures of program costs and service delivery.

In my experience, the simplest evaluation systems are likely to be the best. The performance measures of interest to policymakers may be very simple; in fact, the resulting evaluation system may not even be perceived as an evaluation system. Whenever systematic measurements are made to provide valid, reliable indicators of program performance, an evaluation system exists, whether it measures inputs, program activities, outputs, or impacts—whether it is perceived as an evaluation system or not.

Notes

1. See Joseph S. Wholey et al., *Federal Evaluation Policy* (Washington: The Urban Institute, 1970); Garth N. Buchanan and Joseph S. Wholey, "Federal Level Evaluation," *Evaluation* 1, no. 1 (Fall 1972):17-22; Harry P. Hatry, Richard E. Winnie, and Donald M. Fisk, *Practical Program Evaluation for State and Local Government Officials* (Washington: The Urban Institute, 1973); Pamela Horst et al., "Program Management and the Federal Evaluator," *Public Administration Review* 34, no. 4 (July/August 1974):300-308; John D. Waller et al., *Monitoring for Government Agencies* (Washington: The Urban Institute, 1976); and Richard E. Schmidt et al., *Serving the Federal Evaluation Market* (Washington: The Urban Institute, 1977).

2. See Pamela Horst et al., "Program Management and the Federal Evaluator"; and Joseph S. Wholey et al., "Evaluation: When Is It Really Needed?" *Evaluation*, 2, no. 2 (1975):89-93.

3. Arlington County, Virginia, "Affirmative Action Plan for Equal Employment Opportunity," revised draft, October 11, 1972; adopted by the Arlington County Board, October 18, 1972.

7 Long-Range Planning

As urban America becomes more complex and governments are called upon to meet ever-greater challenges without bankrupting either themselves or the taxpayers, day-to-day government as usual is insufficient to preserve and improve our quality of life. Systematic long-range planning is required to analyze the problems we face, formulate realistic goals and objectives, and select programs that will achieve those objectives efficiently.

Long-range planning looks beyond the problems of the day and those of the upcoming budget, allowing the busy policymaker time to reexamine assumptions, chart new directions, and plan the implementing actions needed to achieve sustained progress toward the better community that all of us seek.

Long-range planning provides a hospitable environment for zero-base budgeting and program evaluation. Zero-base budgeting contributes most to efficient, effective government when done with a multiyear perspective on program costs and benefits; program evaluation both benefits from and contributes to effective long-range planning.

This chapter first touches on the relationships between zero-base budgeting and long-range planning and then shows how program evaluation contributes to effective long-range planning and policy development.

Zero-Base Budgeting and Long-Range Planning

The link between zero-base budgeting and long-range planning is clear and direct. Since it often requires two or more years to achieve substantial savings by redirecting government activities, multiyear objectives and priorities provide better opportunities for effective zero-base budgeting than does a focus only on next year's budget. Further, many of the program analyses required for informed zero-base budgeting cannot be completed in a single budget cycle. One budget cycle identifies the need to analyze the performance of existing programs and program alternatives; these analyses can then be used in subsequent zero-base reviews. Zero-base budgeting is thus itself a way of accomplishing and implementing multiyear planning.

Portions of the material in this chapter first appeared in Joseph S. Wholey, "Using Performance Measures in Long-Range Planning and Policy Formulation," *The Bureaucrat* 5, no. 1 (April 1976):65-86. This material is reprinted by permission of the publisher, Sage Publications, Inc.

Systematic long-range planning provides two additional benefits to zero-base budgeting: (1) clearer identification of goals, objectives, and priorities; and (2) more information on program performance. By more clearly identifying goals, objectives, and priorities, long-range planning provides a sharper focus for subsequent zero-base budget reviews. By assembling existing program-performance information and generating additional program-evaluation work, long-range planning improves the information base for zero-base budgeting.

Program Evaluation and Long-Range Planning

Chapters 4 and 6 indicated that the selection of goals, objectives, and measures of success by policymakers is crucial to effective program evaluation. Long-range planning results in goals, objectives, and priorities. Long-range planning also creates a setting in which policymakers take the time to understand and use evaluation work, both understanding and using past evaluations and commissioning and using new evaluations in the long-range planning process. To the extent that long-range planning supplies these prerequisites for useful evaluation work, it facilitates and supports evaluation. Conversely, program evaluation enhances the feasibility and effectiveness of long-range planning, providing information policymakers need to define problems, analyze program alternatives, set realistic goals and objectives, and select policies and programs that have a high probability of success.

Arlington's Long Range County Improvement Program illustrates both how long-range planning provides opportunities for useful program evaluation work and how program evaluation supports long-range planning. In March 1973 the Arlington County Board initiated Arlington's Long Range County Improvement Program, a comprehensive effort to look ahead, see what Arlington could be like, and help bring about the public and private actions needed to make Arlington a more desirable place to live in the 1970s, the 1980s, and beyond. The board stated:

The Long Range County Improvement Program will set forth, in each area of County responsibility, goals for improving the quality of life of Arlington residents, the highest priority programs for meeting those goals, and the principal steps to be taken to achieve them over the next five to ten years. . . . It will be revised each year and extended forward an additional year. . . . Following formal public hearings a Long Range County Improvement Program . . . will be approved by the County Board as a guide for public policies and planning, County and school administration, and development generally.[1]

A citizen's committee was charged with responsibility for developing the Long Range County Improvement Program. The committee was successively broadened to include members of the county board, school board, planning commission, fiscal affairs advisory committee, growth patterns committee, and representatives of community groups including the chamber of commerce, the board of realtors, and the commission on aging. I chaired the committee and drafted the committee reports mentioned later.

More than a "goals" effort, the Long Range County Improvement Program was conceived as an effort to plan for the future of an existing community in somewhat the same way as planners and developers plan for "new towns." "Goals for Dallas," "Goals for Los Angeles" and, in particular, "Greater Hartford Process" also provided inspiration for Arlington's long-range planning efforts to develop a long-term growth policy, transportation policy, social goals, and public finance and tax policies.[2] We recognized, however, that "goals" efforts in many communities had failed to provide adequately for the resources and follow-up effort required to translate community aspirations into concrete achievements.

The committee on the Long Range Improvement Program used program-evaluation processes and results to identify realistic objectives and effective policies in four broad program areas: growth, housing, and economic development; transportation; social programs; and public finance.

Growth, Housing, and Economic Development

The Problem. In communities throughout the county, residents and their governments are grappling with questions related to growth, housing, development, tax levels, and the quality of life. Much of the work of the committee on the Long Range County Improvement Program and its staff focused on attempts to formulate a *growth policy* for Arlington: objectives for the amount and distribution of future population, jobs, housing units, commercial development, "open space" for park and recreation use, and county actions that would help achieve these objectives. Over the past several years, residents of Arlington had become increasingly concerned about the financial, environmental, and social consequences of growth. Since 1960 Arlington has absorbed a large amount of high-density development and has been increasingly affected by pressures to serve auto commuters. Construction of METRO, the Washington area subway system, was expected to create intensified pressures for development, particularly in the Crystal City and Rosslyn-Ballston areas in which Arlington's subway lines are being constructed. Arlington's long-range planning effort was triggered by planning commission proposals for development of a sewer system to serve twice the community's present population and proposals to allow construction of 30-story buildings near the subway lines.

Residents were also concerned about loss of enrollment in Arlington's public school system, about the fact that many of the shopping areas were declining in sales and attractiveness, that housing prices and rents were increasing rapidly, and that local government costs were rising faster than residents' incomes.

Formulation of Growth Alternatives and a Recommended Growth Policy. Using available local records, U.S. Census data, and the results of a special household survey, consultants and county staff brought together significant data on trends in Arlington's land use, population and employment, household size, public school enrollment, per capita and family incomes, transportation, and government costs (see Exhibit 7-1). Next, five feasible growth policies were examined (Existing Zoning, Moderate Development, High-Density Residential, High Density, and Slow Growth), and projections were made of likely development, population, employment, open-space demands, peak-hour traffic generated, government costs, and government revenues under each of the five alternatives (see Exhibit 7-2).

The analysis revealed that under reasonable assumptions based on present county policies, revenue from new development would tend to reduce the burden on individual Arlington taxpayers. An evaluation of the impact of past development in the Rosslyn and Crystal City areas of Arlington reinforced these conclusions and helped rebut widespread but mistaken citizens beliefs that high-density development costs more in services than the tax revenues it provides.[3] The citizens' committee concluded that new office and commercial development would strengthen the local tax base and reduce individual tax burdens but could further transform Arlington from a primarily residential community into a major employment center.

Using the data on projected population, employment, and associated impacts, including government costs and revenues, but also impressed by community support for housing and shopping close to the planned METRO subway stations, the committee recommended a growth policy that would encourage limited amounts of residential, commercial, and office development within walking distance of METRO subway stations. The committee explicitly agreed to give up the maximum possible net revenue, which would have resulted from concentration on office and commercial development, and instead recommended a balanced mix of new jobs and new housing supply to "avoid night-time office canyon 'ghost towns,' encourage commuter use of public transportation, provide walk-to-walk opportunities, and reduce suburban sprawl."[4]

Growth-policy objectives were proposed in terms of population; public school enrollment; in-county employment; residential, hotel, office, and commercial development; and open space for parks and recreation (see Exhibit 7-3); as well as moderate-income housing, residents' opinions of their neighborhoods, retail trade, and hotel and restaurant sales.

Conclusions. Analyses of existing data (including an evaluation of county costs and revenues associated with high-density development over the past 15 years) and analyses of the consequences of several development alternatives made it

Exhibit 7-1
Trend Data

Land Use

	1960	1974	Percent Change
Residential (Units)	55,900	72,700	+29
Single Family	28,600	30,600	+7
Condominium	0	1,740	NA
Multi-Family	27,300	42,100	+54
Garden Apts.	21,400	23,800	+11
High Rise Apts.	5,900	17,000	+188
Condominium	0	1,340	NA
Office (Square Feet)	600,000	12,765,000	+2028
Low Rise	600,000	1,598,000	+166
High Rise	0	11,167,000	NA
Hotel (Rooms)	1,840	5,400	+193
Vacant Land (Acres)	1,000	640	−36

Population and Employment

	1960	1970	Percent Change
Households	54,500	69,400	+27
Married Couples	39,400	38,500	−2
Married Couples with Children under 18	21,800	17,500	−20
Children under 18	49,100	41,600	−15
Public School Children	25,200	20,100[a]	−20
Adults 55 and Older	22,500	33,100	+47
Persons per Household	2.9	2.4	−16
Per Capita Income (1970 dollars)	$3,900	$5,400	+39
Family Income (1970 dollars)	$11,100	$13,700	+24
Jobs	104,200[b]	129,600[c]	+24
Jobs in Arlington held by nonresidents	67,700[b]	81,600[c]	+21

Transportation

Auto Use (vehicles per day)	1960	1974	Percent Change
At Alexandria/Fairfax Border	265,000	506,000[d]	+91
At Potomac Bridges	265,000	335,000	+26

Bus Ridership (peak hour)	1968	1974	Percent Change
At Alexandria/Fairfax Border	14,800	16,300	+11
At Potomac Bridges	11,300	12,000	+6

Source: "Planning for Arlington's Future: Some Critical Choices," Arlington County, Spring 1975.

[a]1974 enrollment   [c]1974 figures
[b]1965 figures   [d]1973 figures

94

Exhibit 7-2
Implications of Development Alternatives (Possibilities)

	1974	Existing Zoning	I: Moderate Development	II: High Density Res.	III: High Density	Slow Growth
			Year 2000			
Land Use						
Total Residential (Units)	72,800	86,000	92,000	113,200	105,000	77,000
Crystal City Area	9,200	17,600	21,000	26,700	22,300	NA
Rosslyn-Ballston	12,100	12,800	15,600	30,900	27,600	NA
Balance of County	51,500	55,600	55,600	55,600	55,600	NA
High-Rise Apartments	17,000	25,100	31,600	54,700	47,200	18,700
Crystal City Area	5,400	13,500	16,900	22,600	18,200	NA
Rosslyn-Ballston	3,700	3,700	6,800	24,200	21,100	NA
Balance of County	7,900	7,900	7,900	7,900	7,900	NA
Hotel (Rooms)	4,200	7,100	7,300	7,500	8,900	6,200
Crystal City Area	2,300	3,900	3,200	2,400	3,800	NA
Rosslyn-Ballston	1,300	1,300	2,100	2,400	3,100	NA
Balance of County	600	2,000	2,000	2,000	2,000	NA
Commercial/Office (Square Feet)	22,500,000	39,700,000	37,300,000	33,900,000	41,200,000	25,600,000
Crystal City Area	7,500,000	12,100,000	10,600,000	10,100,000	12,600,000	NA
Rosslyn-Ballston	9,800,000	18,100,000	17,200,000	14,300,000	19,100,000	NA
Balance of County	5,200,000	9,500,000	9,500,000	9,500,000	9,500,000	NA
High-Rise Office (Sq. Ft.)	11,200,000	20,500,000	20,100,000	18,700,000	25,800,000	12,800,000
Crystal City Area	5,600,000	9,900,000	8,400,000	7,900,000	9,700,000	NA
Rosslyn-Ballston	5,400,000	8,600,000	9,700,000	8,800,000	14,100,000	NA
Balance of County	200,000	2,000,000	2,000,000	2,000,000	2,000,000	NA
School Buildings	39	30	30	30	30	30
Population and Employment						
Population	174,000	192,000	200,400	231,500	220,800	180,000
Crystal City Area	17,100	28,700	33,500	41,400	35,300	NA
Rosslyn-Ballston	22,200	22,300	25,900	49,100	44,500	NA

Balance of County	134,700	141,000	141,000	141,000	141,000	NA
Public School Enrollment	20,500	16,500	16,500	16,800	16,600	16,100
Crystal City Area	1,500	1,500	1,500	1,600	1,500	NA
Rosslyn-Ballston	1,800	1,700	1,700	1,900	1,800	NA
Balance of County	17,200	13,300	13,300	13,300	13,300	NA
Employment	133,700	208,000	197,500	182,400	214,200	147,000
Crystal City Area	31,800	51,900	45,300	42,900	53,400	NA
Rosslyn-Ballston	42,000	78,400	74,500	61,800	83,100	NA
Balance of County	716	791	813	879	852	716
Open-Space Demands	55	92	107	132	113	NA
Crystal City Area	40	40	47	88	80	NA
Rosslyn-Ballston	721	659	659	659	659	NA
Balance of County	103,000	125,000	124,300	129,400	136,900	107,000
Peak-Hour Trips Generated	20,700	29,800	29,100	31,000	33,200	NA
Crystal City Area	28,500	36,800	37,100	40,000	45,300	NA
Rosslyn-Ballston	54,800	58,400	58,400	58,400	58,400	NA
Costs						
County Revenues	$95,800,000	$138,700,000	$138,800,000	$150,300,000	$155,400,000	$116,000,000
Crystal City Area	14,700,000	28,500,000	28,500,000	31,300,000	32,700,000	NA
Rosslyn-Ballston	20,500,000	31,800,000	31,900,000	40,600,000	44,300,000	NA
Balance of County	60,600,000	78,400,000	78,400,000	78,400,000	78,400,000	NA
County Costs (Including Schools)	93,000,000	151,500,000	153,800,000	165,200,000	164,700,000	134,800,000
Crystal City Area	9,400,000	21,700,000	22,900,000	26,200,000	24,900,000	NA
Rosslyn-Ballston	11,700,000	22,700,000	23,800,000	31,900,000	32,700,000	NA
Balance of County	71,900,000	107,100,000	107,100,000	107,100,000	107,100,000	NA
School Costs	36,500,000	43,300,000	43,500,000	44,100,000	43,600,000	42,300,000
Surplus/Deficit	2,800,000	−12,800,000	−15,000,000	−14,900,000	−9,300,000	−18,800,000
Crystal City Area	5,300,000	6,700,000	5,600,000	5,000,000	7,800,000	NA
Rosslyn-Ballston	8,800,000	9,200,000	8,200,000	8,700,000	11,600,000	NA
Balance of County	−11,300,000	−28,700,000	−28,700,000	−28,700,000	−287,000,000	NA
Surplus/Deficit per Resident	+15	−65	−75	−65	−40	−105

Source: "Planning for Arlington's Future: Some Critical Choices," Arlington County, Spring 1975.

Exhibit 7-3
Recommended Growth Policy

By the years 1980 and 2000, the committee recommends that Arlington County aim for the following distribution of population, jobs, housing units, commercial development, and open space, and the following improvements in retail, hotel, and restaurant trade:

Population and Employment

	1974	2000	Percent Change
Population	165,000[a]	210,000-215,000	27-30
Crystal City Area	16,000	31,000	94
Rosslyn-Ballston	21,000	40,000-45,000	90-114
Balance of County	128,000	139,000	9
Public School Enrollment	20,500	18,700	−9
Crystal City Area	1,500	2,000	25
Rosslyn-Ballston	1,800	2,400	33
Balance of County	17,200	14,300	−17
Employment	154,000	207,500	35
Crystal City Area	32,000	45,500	42
Rosslyn-Ballston	43,700	66,000	51
Balance of County	78,300	96,000	23

Land Use

	1974	1980	2000
Residential (Units)	72,800		104,600-107,600
Crystal City Area	9,200		21,000
Rosslyn-Ballston	12,100		27,000-30,000
Balance of County	51,500		56,600
Units with 3 or more Bedrooms	23,072		29,000
Hotel (Rooms)	4,200		8,900
Crystal City Area	2,300		3,800
Rosslyn-Ballston	1,300		3,100
Balance of County	600		2,000
Office (Thousands of square feet)	12,765		−
Crystal City Area	5,660		9,300
Rosslyn-Ballston	6,486		10,500
Balance of County	614		−
Commercial (Thousands of square feet)	9,698		−
Retail	4,798		−
Crystal City Area	202		1,300
Rosslyn-Ballston	2,212		2,700-3,200
Balance of County	2,384		−
Service	3,543		−
Other	1,356		−

Exhibit 7-3 (cont.)

Open Space (acres)	716	804	940
Crystal City Area	55	70	92
Rosslyn-Ballston	40	69	115
Balance of County	621	665	733

Source: *Planning for Arlington's Future: A Long Range County Improvement Program*, Arlington County, July 1975.

[a]The best current data indicate that Arlington's average household size continues to decline rapidly and that Arlington's 1974 population was no more than 165,000.

possible for the committee to recommend a specific growth policy. These analyses and evaluations allowed selection of a growth policy designed to balance new jobs with new residents, improve shopping areas, provide new park and recreation areas, and preserve the residential character of the community, while capitalizing on the economic development opportunities represented by major local, state, and federal investments in public transportation. On the basis of a separate analysis, the committee further recommended a tourism-development program to attract visitors to Arlington hotels and restaurants.

Explicit attention to tradeoffs and to areas in which county action would have little effect (e.g., traffic on local streets is dominated by metropolitan-area travel and would be only slightly affected by the amount or type of development in Arlington) helped a diverse committee to reach consensus on a recommended course of action.

The recommended growth policy was accepted by the county board with some modifications. The adopted growth policy then became the basis for a series of changes in the county's master land-use plan and a series of zoning actions that together are implementing the county's adopted growth policy (again, with some modifications). It is clear that problems related to the national economy may make it difficult to attract private capital in the short term; there already are encouraging signs, however, that major land owners will undertake specific development projects after a growth policy is adopted. In addition, a planned monitoring system will make it possible for Arlington to keep track of progress, or lack of progress, toward growth objectives and to revise its growth policy when indicated.

Transportation

The Problem. As in cities and suburbs throughout the country, Arlington residents have become increasingly disturbed by traffic congestion and air pollution. New highway construction threatens existing homes and neighborhoods. At the same time, subsidies for public transportation have become a rapidly growing burden on local taxpayers. Concerns over the disruption caused by auto traffic, parking, and auto-related air pollution clash with growing alarm over the rising costs of public transportation.

Formulation of Transportation Alternatives and a Recommended Transportation Policy. The committee examined trends in auto trips into and through Arlington; public transportation ridership, costs, income from the fare box, and taxpayer subsidies; and findings of research and evaluation studies on the effects of changes in fares and service levels.[5] Direct and indirect subsidies to private auto commuters were also estimated.

Committee members then analyzed (1) the effects of alternative bus fares on peak-hour bus ridership; (2) the effects of more convenient, faster bus service, such as express buses operating on reserved or preferential bus lanes; and (3) the possibility of substituting dial-a-ride or lower-cost shared taxi service for some of the less-productive night-time and weekend bus service (see Exhibit 7-4). The available data revealed, for example, that revenue from peak-hour bus fare increases could greatly reduce taxpayer subsidies without having much effect on peak-hour bus ridership.

Data from public opinion surveys revealed overwhelming support for increasing taxes to improve public transportation and reduce fares, and identified the sales tax as the "fairest" tax in the minds of local residents.

Committee analyses took place in the context of Arlington County and Northern Virginia efforts to raise bus fares and efforts to "rationalize" the bus routes established by a number of different bus companies prior to public acquisition of the bus lines. Major factors considered by committee members included:

The rapidly increasing costs of public transportation

The costs of traffic, parking, and air pollution

Public reactions against proposed construction and widening of county streets and highways

National data demonstrating the relatively small effect of fare increases in peak-hour bus ridership

National and local census data showing that peak-hour bus riders have incomes approximately the same as those of local taxpayers

Data showing that bus service improvements in Northern Virginia were building ridership

Data showing the benefits of increased car-pooling

Survey data on local residents' support for increased funding for public transportation, both rail and bus.

The recommended transportation policy focused on increased use of public transportation, car pools, and taxis; the minimizing of vehicle miles traveled; and actions to reduce the impact of transportation on the county taxpayer.

Exhibit 7-4
Transportation Costs and Ridership

Metrobus: Approximate Systemwide Costs, Fares, and
Taxpayer Subsidies[a]

	FY 1974	FY 1975 (est)	FY 1976 (est)
Average cost/rider	70¢	80¢	90¢
Average fare/rider	50¢	50¢	50¢
Taxpayer subsidy/rider	20¢	30¢	40d
Cost to Arlington taxpayers	$2,000,000	$4,000,000	$6,000,000

Approximate Impact of Alternative Bus Fares on Peak-
Hour Bus Ridership and Fiscal Year 1976 Taxpayer Subsidies[a]

Basic peak hour bus fare (one zone)	30¢	40¢ (present level)	50¢	60¢
Change in peak-hour bus ridership[b]	+2.5%	0	−2.5%	−5%
Cost to Arlington taxpayers	$8,000,000	$6,000,000	$4,000,000	$2,000,000

Approximate Costs, Fares, and Taxpayer Subsidies[a]

	Metrobus Virginia Lines (FY 1975)				Door-to-Door	
	Weekday		Saturday	Sunday	Dial-a-bus	Shared taxi
	Peak	Off-peak				
Cost/hour	$30.00	$20.00	$20.00	$20.00	$16.00	$9.00
Average cost/rider	.85	1.20	1.00	1.50	2.00-3.00	1.50
Average fare/rider	.65	.55	.55	.55	.25-.50	.50-1.50
Taxpayer subsidy/rider	.20	.65	.45	.95	1.50-2.75	0-1.00

Source: "Planning for Arlington's Future: Some Critical Choices," Arlington County, Spring 1975.

[a]These figures are not precise but do illustrate the general relationships among operating costs, fares, and taxpayer subsidies.

[b]For every 1 percent change in bus fares, the changes in peak-hour bus ridership would probably be between 0.05 and 0.25 percent, with the actual change likely to be approximately 0.1 percent.

The committee recommended county board adoption or reaffirmation of a number of transportation goals, including prompt completion of the proposed Metrorail system; establishment and enforcement of reserved and preferential bus lanes to upgrade peak-hour bus service; testing demand-responsive public transportation, including lower-cost shared taxi, dial-a-ride, and jitney service to complement/supplement mass transit; and actions to discourage single-passenger auto commuting to and through Arlington.

Recommended county objectives were stated in terms of proportion of work trips by public transit, car-pooling, peak-hour auto work trips, vehicle miles traveled, on-time reliability of bus service, mass transit ridership, commuter traffic on neighborhood streets, numbers of miles of reserved/preferential bus lanes, and shared-taxi ridership (see Exhibit 7-5).

The committee also recommended several actions to minimize the impact of transportation on the local tax base, e.g., increased federal and state funding of capital costs, periodic adjustments of Metrobus fares to ensure that they cover at least two-thirds of operating costs, examination of the feasibility of setting Metrorail fares high enough to cover all operating costs, an areawide taxing authority for the mass transit system, improvements in bus system operating efficiency, and restrictions on the amount of land devoted to new highways and parking lots.

Exhibit 7-5
Recommended Transportation Objectives

1. By the years 1980 and 1992, the committee recommends that Arlington aim for the following proportions of work trips carried by public transportation and car pools in and through Arlington:

	1968	1980	1992
Work Trips	100%	100%	100%
Work Trips by Transit	22%	26%	36%
Work Trips by Auto	78%	74%	64%
Persons/Vehicle	1.3	1.4	1.6
(Total Trips)	(365,600)	–	(607,600)
(Transit Trips)	(80,400)	–	(218,700)
(Auto Trips in and through Arlington)	(285,200)	–	(388,900)
(Autos Used)	(219,400)	–	(243,100)

2. Minimize vehicle miles traveled.

3. Improve the on-time reliability of Metrobus service.

4. Increase public ridership of Metro, peak and off-peak.

5. Reduce commuter traffic on neighborhood streets.

6. Increase miles of reserved/preferential bus lanes, sidewalks, and bicycle trails.

7. Increase shared-taxi ridership.

Source: *Planning for Arlington's Future: A Long Range County Improvement Program* Arlington County, July 1975.

Moreover, costs of public transportation were rising so rapidly that the committee recommended both a fare increase during peak commuting hours and state legislation to permit a regional 1 percent sales tax for public transportation.

Conclusions. In large measure, the committee's proposed transportation policy represented reaffirmation or provided a sharper formulation of past county policies. The committee recognized that, as a small community in a large metropolitan area, Arlington had to try to influence transportation mainly through actions of regional and state bodies. Arlington County and Northern Virginia have since been successful in obtaining bus fare increases in peak hours (which have been implemented in Northern Virginia with relatively little effect on bus ridership). Several actions have also been taken to reduce or consolidate little-used night-time and weekend bus service. Adoption of a county transportation policy has directed elected officials' and staff efforts toward specific objectives and helped Arlington to influence metropolitan-area transportation policies and programs.

Social Goals

The Problem. Like governments at all levels, the Arlington County Board faces a potentially endless demand for public services, limited by public unwillingness to pay higher taxes. As across the nation, in recent years larger proportions of Arlington residents' incomes have been spent on local public services.

Much of the committee's work on social programs reflected responses to input from county board advisory committees, community groups, and individuals—including data from the committee's household survey. In household surveys, residents placed highest priority on crime control and improvements in the criminal justice system, as well as on preserving and improving Arlington neighborhoods, improving job opportunities, improving Arlington's educational system, and improving life for elderly residents. Many citizens also noted that existing communications (public information) programs are inadequate.

Formulation of Goals and Objectives. In formulating recommended social goals, the committee and other county board advisory committees used data on reported crime, special surveys on needs for nursing homes and residences for deinstitutionalized mentally ill and mentally retarded people, data on student achievement levels and on the numbers of non-English-speaking children enrolled in the public schools, results of a special survey of the demand for preschool child care programs, data on proportions of citizens not aware of existing county services, and data on the amount and distribution of park and recreation facilities. Recommended social goals (Exhibit 7-6) were stated in terms of reported crime, citizens' feeling of security, numbers of nursing home beds,

Exhibit 7-6
Recommended Social Goals

1. Reduce reported rates or robbery, aggravated assaults, and burglary by 20 percent, over the next 5 years.

2. Improve neighborhood security. Increase the proportion of citizens who feel safe walking alone at night to 95 percent, over the next 5 years.

3. Increase the number of nursing home beds in Arlington to 800 by 1980, and to 1200 by the year 2000.

4. Provide improved community mental health and mental retardation services, including group homes and follow-up services for former mental patients such as those being discharged from state hospitals under the accelerated deinstitutionalization program.

Develop group homes and apartment clusters for 100 mentally retarded or mentally ill adults by 1980.

5. Improve students' mathematics, writing, and reading achievements.

Reduce the proportion of pupils reading (or computing) below grade level. Request the school board to develop specific attainable objectives both countywide and school-by-school, especially for students who have been in the Arlington public schools for at least two or three years.

6. Increase the number of children (age 2-21) with handicaps being served by the public schools.

7. Provide English for speakers of other languages (ESOL) to 100 percent of children in need of such services by 1980:

	1974	1980
Students who speak English as a second language	1561	X
(a) Functional in English	Y_1	X_1
(b) Not functional in English	Y_2	X_2
Students in the ESOL program	650	Z
Z/X_2	—	100%

8. Encourage establishment of child care services for 100 percent of children in need of such care by 1980.

	1974	1980
Estimated number of households with children under six years of age who want and would use child care services if available.	6242 8235	X
Percent who would use child care services if available.	73.5%	Y
Percent now using child care programs.	26.5%	Z
Z/Y	36.0%	100%

9. Reduce the proportions of citizens not aware of public services:

	1974	1980
Tax Relief and Rent Relief		
General Population	63%	30%
Elderly Residents	37%	15%
Lower-Cost Shared Taxi Service	99%(?)	50%

Source: *Planning for Arlington's Future: A Long Range County Improvement Program*, Arlington County, July 1975.

numbers of group homes for mentally retarded or mentally ill adults, students' mathematics and reading achievement, numbers of handicapped children served by the public schools, proportions of foreign students provided English-language training, proportions of preschool children provided child care services, and proportions of citizens not aware of public services.

Conclusions. In the area of social programs, where much less evaluation and analysis was done than in growth and transportation, recommended goals and objectives more nearly constituted a "wish list." The committee believed that county board adoption of specific objectives and monitoring of progress toward them would tend to make major county programs more productive and more accountable. In fact, board adoption of specific objectives resulted in subsequent actions to attract two additional nursing homes to Arlington, establishment of a system of group homes for mentally ill or mentally retarded adults, adoption of an updated Child Care Ordinance, provision of sliding-scale subsidies for children in private child care centers, and specific efforts to develop a new Building Security Ordinance.

Public Finance

The Problem. Over the past 20 years, Arlington County expenditures for public services have risen sharply, though less rapidly than in other jurisdictions. A major reason for Arlington's long-range planning was the desire to have a full understanding of the long-range financial consequences of current choices. It quickly became clear that, if current trends continued, Arlington would require significantly more revenue simply to provide existing levels of services.

Formulation of Public Finance Goals. The committee, staff, and consultants assembled data on the revenue options currently available and other options proposed by staff and citizens. Surveys of residents and discussions at community meetings revealed broad support for five propositions:

1. Economic development should be pursued, to broaden the tax base.
2. The local tax structure should be made fairer (i.e., less regressive).
3. Those who benefit from special services should bear the costs of those services.
4. Additional taxes should be levied to improve public transportation and reduce fares.
5. The sales tax is (considered) the fairest and least burdensome tax.

After examining these data, the committee responded by recommending:

1. Economic development efforts, as outlined earlier.
2. Changes in tax rates and transfer payments to remove or correct regressive features in the existing tax system.

3. State legislation to allow substitution of a local income tax for some existing local taxes.
4. Imposition of user charges to finance costs of many public services.
5. State legislation to allow a sales tax for public transportation.

Conclusions. Though measurable objectives were not stated in the public finance area (the major goal seeming to be a balanced budget every year!), attention to quantitative measures of tax incidence and of residents' perceptions promoted consensus on desirable county tax policies. Quantitative data on the regressiveness of the local tax structure supported subsequent efforts to expand Arlington's tax relief and housing expense relief programs; the emphasis on user charges supported subsequent efforts to impose or raise user fees to finance at least part of the costs of specialized services that benefit relatively small numbers of users. The county has (so far unsuccessfully) supported efforts to persuade the state legislature to authorize a sales tax or local income tax whose proceeds would fund public transportation programs.

Results of Program Evaluation and Long-Range Planning

Based on what we have learned about government, it is clear that one of the most crucial and most difficult challenges is getting public action directed at realistic, measurable objectives. In the Long Range County Improvement Program, Arlington County reviewed major areas of government responsibility, using a combination of citizen input, program evaluation, and program analysis, and developed a set of recommended objectives, programs, and ways to monitor progress toward objectives. Information provided by the committee raised the level of informed debate over community growth, transportation, and tax policies.

In December 1975, after a series of three informational meetings for the general public, two county board work sessions, and two public hearings, "... [the] County Board adopted the bulk of the Committee's recommendations as the official Long Range County Improvement Program, with specific amendments stemming from the prior work sessions, public hearings, and written comments submitted to the Board."[6] Since December 1975, even after the composition of the county board changed from five Democrats to three Democrats and two Republicans,[7] the goals, objectives, and priorities in the Long Range County Improvement Program have guided county board and staff policies and actions.

Growth, Housing, Economic Development. County actions to implement the Long Range County Improvement Program include adoption of a revised land-use plan guided by, and generally consistent with, the county board's adopted growth policy; rezonings and site plans to promote the type of development specified in the Long Range County Improvement Program; revision of the zoning ordinance to implement the adopted growth policy; initiation of economic development and tourism development programs; adoption of a Historic District Ordinance designed to help preserve structures and sites of historical interest; obtaining state legislation clarifying Arlington's ability to establish special-benefit tax districts to finance public improvements in the vicinity of METRO subway stations; and expansion of county and federal rent supplement programs and other programs to promote moderate-income housing.

Transportation. County and regional action to implement the Long Range County Improvement Program transportation policies include efforts to improve the speed and reliability of bus service, testing of different types of demand-responsive public transportation service, increases in METRO fares and consolidation of little-used night-time and weekend bus service, and approval and partial implementation of specific plans and programs to complete needed sidewalks and a planned 80-mile network of hiking and biking trails.

Social Programs. Other significant county actions to implement the Long Range County Improvement Program include the drafting of a Building Security Ordinance to make residences and businesses less vulnerable to burglary; establishment of a hospital and nursing home commission, lease of county-owned property for a privately operated nursing home, and zoning action to ensure construction of another nursing home; development of a comprehensive residential system for mentally ill and mentally retarded residents; and adoption of an updated Child Care Ordinance and establishment of sliding-scale subsidies for children in private child care centers.

Public Finance. Significant county actions to implement the county's long-range financial goals include those related to growth and economic development; adoption of zero-base budgeting; expanded user charges for discretionary public services; expansion of county tax relief and rent supplement programs for the elderly, the disabled, and needy working families with children; establishment of a federally funded Housing Assistance Program; state legislation expanding the county's authority to use special-benefit tax districts to finance public improvements needed in the vicinity of METRO subway stations; expanded enforcement of county taxes; adoption of Arlington's first five-year capital-improvement program; and return to annual budgeting for capital improvements rather than completely relying on bond issues to finance them.

The Long Range County Improvement Program has done much to make Arlington's government more efficient and more effective. Program evaluation provided significant support to these long-range planning efforts and is expected to provide periodic progress reports as long-range plans and policies are implemented and updated.

Notes

1. See *Planning for Arlington's Future: A Long Range County Improvement Program*, Arlington County, July 1975; and "Planning for Arlington's Future: Some Critical Choices," Arlington County, Spring 1975. These two reports were prepared by myself as chairman of the Committee on the Long-Range County Improvement Program. Important inputs to the committee include an Arlington County staff report, *Critical Choices for Arlington*, Arlington County, March 1975; and two consultant reports by Peat, Marwick, Mitchell, and Company, *Rosslyn/Crystal City Impact Analysis*, Washington, May 1974, and *Transit Station Impact Analysis*, Washington, December 1974.

2. See, in particular, American City Corporation, *The Greater Hartford Process*, Columbia, Maryland, April 1972.

3. Peat, Marwick, Mitchell, and Company, *Rosslyn/Crystal City Impact Analysis*, Washington, May 1974.

4. *Planning for Arlington's Future: A Long Range County Improvement Program*, Arlington County, July 1975.

5. Ronald Kirby and Michael Kemp, members of the Urban Institute's Transportation Research staff, provided a good deal of information summarizing past research; Tom Breuer of the Northern Virginia Transportation Commission staff provided very useful local and regional data.

6. See *A Long Range County Improvement Program: Goals, Objectives and Priorities*, Arlington County, December 1975.

7. All the present county board members actually campaigned for election as independents, running with the endorsements of political parties and of other community groups.

8 Improving Government Efficiency and Effectiveness

I started with the premise that better performance is needed at all levels of government. I inquired into the possibility that some form of zero-base budgeting and some form of program evaluation might help policymakers make government more efficient and effective. What, then, are the costs and benefits of the zero-base budgeting and program evaluation processes examined here? What is the outlook for improving government performance with the help of these policy tools?

Costs

Zero-base budgeting and program evaluation processes impose significant costs on policymakers and managers. Policymakers, managers, and their top staff members are forced to examine the consequences of existing program activities, as well as of program alternatives, and to clarify objectives and measures of success.

In comparison with other zero-base budgeting and program evaluation processes, however, our zero-base budgeting and program evaluation processes save time and effort. Paperwork and overhead requirements are minimized; staff activities are concentrated in priority decision areas; and time is made available for substantive dialogue among policymakers, managers, and evaluators.

Paperwork and Resource Commitments Are Minimized

One of the major problems in "traditional" zero-base budgeting is the amount of paperwork and staff time required to prepare and rank decision packages. Our simplified zero-base budgeting process limits preparation of decision packages to decisions required to reduce agency operating levels by (say) 10 or 15 percent, decisions required for selective increases in operating levels, and additional decision packages identified in the initial dialogues between policymakers and managers. By eliminating the ranking of decision packages, our zero-base budgeting process further reduces the required staff report. Similarly, our simplified program-evaluation process limits data collection and analysis to the measurements and comparisons needed by the policymakers and managers for whom the evaluation is being done.

107

Staff Activities Are Concentrated in Priority Decision Areas

Under "traditional" zero-base budgeting and program evaluation practices, decision packages and data are presented in areas often far removed from any realistic likelihood of policy change. As a result, staff activities are spread very thin, and few questions are definitively answered.

Once decision packages and data collection are focused on a relative handful of areas in which decisions are likely, as is the case in the zero-base budgeting and program evaluation processes presented here, staff activities can be concentrated on answering a more manageable number of questions. The ensuing dialogues further focus the area of staff inquiry, more efficiently using the staff time available.

Time is Made Available for More Substantive Dialogue
among Policymakers, Managers, and Evaluators

In the "traditional" zero-base budgeting approach, the volume of decision packages to be analyzed results in heavy reliance on budget staff to interact with managers, to consolidate decision packages to reduce the volume of information actually reaching policymakers, and to interact with the policymakers as they make their decisions. By reducing the number of decision packages prepared, the simplified zero-base budgeting process makes it possible for substantive dialogue to take place between policymakers and managers, limiting the influence of the budget staff and promoting agreements between policymakers and managers on activities to be undertaken and objectives to be achieved.

In "traditional" program evaluation, there is relatively little contact between policymakers and evaluators. Under our program-evaluation approach, however, the evaluator provides intermediate products, presenting policymakers' and managers' intentions, the feasibility of measuring progress toward objectives, preliminary evaluation results, and ongoing indicators of progress—using each product as the occasion for dialogue clarifying what the policymaker really needs to know about program activities and results.

Benefits

Our zero-base budgeting and program-evaluation tools allow policymakers to understand the consequences of policy choices, gain control of government programs and staff activities, identify lower-priority activities and expenditures, and concentrate resources on priority objectives.

Understanding the Consequences of Policy Choices

For the policymaker, as for the individual citizen, it is difficult to know what the government is up to—and even more difficult to have an impact on government activities and performance. Whether policymakers are in the executive or the legislative branch of government, they face a standard set of difficulties. Problems are identified; legislation is passed; programs and agencies are created, staffed, and funded; but the public sees little progress toward solution of the original problems. Once programs are established, both the bureaucracy and other recipients of public funds tend to pursue their own objectives.

To understand government operations and effects, it is necessary for policymakers to know what activities are underway and what would be the consequences of changing those activities. Zero-base budgeting allows policymakers to go as deeply as they wish into the bases of existing programs and staff activities—learning how the bureaucracy would respond to policy changes and how the public would be affected by those changes. By forcing managers to set priorities and identify the consequences of reducing or eliminating lower-priority activities, policymakers set the stage for dialogue and agreement on objectives and performance targets. Given a set of policy/management objectives and performance targets, policymakers are then in a position to monitor the degree of progress toward agreed objectives and to use that information in future policy decisions.

Gaining Control of Government Programs and Staff Activities

Lack of control is a traditional frustration of government policymakers. Zero-base budgeting and program evaluation provide information the policymaker can use to get agreement on priority objectives and activities and to reallocate resources away from lower-priority, less-productive functions.

In both the Arlington County government and the METRO Transit Authority, policymakers gained far greater control of the organization through zero-base budgeting than policymakers had ever achieved using incremental budgeting processes. Policy issues were surfaced and resolved at policy level; lower-priority activities were identified and reduced or eliminated; efficiencies and economies were imposed; new directions were set; resources were freed for application to activities and programs that policymakers considered higher-priority than existing staff functions. Face-to-face dialogue with managers allowed policymakers to communicate, and get agreement on, desired changes.

For the governor, mayor, agency head, or appropriations committee chairman who wishes to make government programs more efficient or to move program activities toward specific objectives, our zero-base budgeting process provides great opportunities. If policymakers have clear objectives and the will to achieve them, monitoring and evaluation can provide reliable information on progress or lack of progress toward objectives and thus lay the basis for policy and management actions that will enhance progress toward objectives.

Identifying Lower-Priority Activities and Expenditures

Given the political realities that exist in most governments, policymakers will have to reallocate existing resources if they are to undertake program expansions and new policy initiatives. Zero-base budgeting and program evaluation provide policymakers with information they can use to justify reduction or elimination of lower-priority programs and activities—thus gaining the opportunity to move in new policy directions, even in the face of limited resources.

The time available to the policymaker typically will not permit him to review all existing operations in detail. As a result, budget decisions are often made based primarily on the *names* of the programs in question. When the program has no name, as is true of most ongoing staff activities, there are no decisions and therefore no reductions in existing levels of activities and expenditures.

By forcing managers to identify their 10, 15, or 50 percent lowest-priority staff activities and expenditures, the policymaker gains real insight into existing operations. Through the ensuing dialogue, the policymaker can identify activities and expenditures that are low priority *both* for the manager and for the policymaker, and thus can learn where to make reductions if reductions have to be made to free resources for higher-priority programs or for tax-rate reductions.

Concentrating Resources on Priority Objectives

The failure to establish clear objectives and priorities is probably the major failing of government organizations. Faced with conflicting demands and inadequate resources, government often accomplishes relatively little progress in *any* direction. Both zero-base budgeting and program evaluation allow the policymaker to establish clear objectives and measures of progress. By setting realistic objectives and selecting the measures of progress that are to be used in assessing program accomplishments, the policymaker gives purpose and direction to the programs for which he is responsible.

Leadership

Informed government leadership can make a difference. Contact with program reality is important; vision and will are essential. Given policymakers with the vision and the will to make government better serve their fellow citizens, zero-base budgeting and program evaluation can help make that leadership effective.

Appendix A:
Arlington County Fiscal
Year 1977 Decision
Packages

This appendix reproduces selected portions of the decision packages considered by the Arlington County Board in its work on the fiscal year 1977 county budget. Decision packages are presented for the police department, the library department, the department of human resources, and the department of property management.

Exhibit A-1

Detailed Activity Decision Package: Police Vandalism Investigation

Page ___6___ of ___29___

No.	Activity Name	Department and/or Division
9002-23	Vandalism	Police

A. Alternative (Different Level of Effort or Different Way of Performance) and Consequences

Alternate Level: 52% of Current Budget: At the proposed level, we recommend that a high percentage of preliminary investigations, which are now conducted on-site by officers in the field, would be conducted by telephone. Follow-up investigations at the current level would be continued, either by Juvenile Section officers or by patrol officers. A factor to be considered in dealing with this crime is that although it is a great nuisance and expense, it does not generate the same feeling of insecurity and fear of crime as does burglary, theft, or robbery.

Reduction ~~or Addition~~ of Positions (List)

Sworn	Civilian	Total
0.81	0.01	0.82

$ Cost Decrease ~~or Increase~~

Personnel	Nonpersonnel	Total
$17,290	$2,710	$20,000
		Revenue Impact
		None

B. Alternative (Different Level of Effort or Different Way of Performance) and Consequences

Reduction or Addition of Positions (List)

$ Cost Decrease or Increase

Personnel	Nonpersonnel	Total
		Revenue Impact

Exhibit A-2

Detailed Activity Decision Package: Police Traffic Patrol

No.	Activity Name	Department and/or Division
9003-10	Traffic Patrol	Police

A. Alternative (Different Level of Effort or Different Way of Performance) and Consequences

Alternate Level: 75% of Current Budget: The proposed alternative level will reduce the deployment of officers engaged in traffic patrol to 75% of the current level, and will have secondary impact on delivery of other related activities, as follows: 9003-20 (accident investigation), and 9003-40 (non-hazardous moving violations). A decision involving traffic patrol activity should therefore be considered in conjunction with the other two activities mentioned above.

Reduction or Addition of Positions (List)

Sworn	Civilian	Total
4.86	0.07	4.93

$ Cost Decrease or Increase

Personnel	Nonpersonnel	Total
$103,569	$11,431	$115,000
		Revenue Impact
		None

B. Alternative (Different Level of Effort or Different Way of Performance) and Consequences

Reduction or Addition of Positions (List)

$ Cost Decrease or Increase

Personnel	Nonpersonnel	Total
		Revenue Impact

Exhibit A-3

Detailed Activity Decision Package: Police Accident Investigation

No.	Activity Name	Department and/or Division
9003-20	Accident Investigation	Police

A. Alternative (Different Level of Effort or Different Way of Performance) and Consequences

Alternate Level: 33% of Current Level: Under this proposed alternative, we will continue to investigate fatal and injury accidents as at present. However, we propose the elimination of most of our effort in property damage accidents. We would continue to go to the scene of property damage accidents to render aid, but in 90% of these accidents we would then leave the scene as soon as traffic problems have been handled. Forms would be given to the drivers, with instructions to mail the report to the department. (At times, such as in severe snow storms, we are forced to suspend property damage accident investigation as per the above, with no great harm done).

We already have a great deal of past experience on file which is used for traffic engineering purposes. By and large, we don't learn anything new from current accident investigation efforts.

This reduction in service will also save a tremendous amount of time spent in court in testimony in accident cases.

Reduction ~~or Addition~~ of Positions (List)

Sworn	Civilian	Total
8.46	0.11	8.57

$ Cost Decrease ~~or Increase~~

Personnel	Nonpersonnel	Total
$180,120	$19,880	$200,000

Revenue Impact
None

B. Alternative (Different Level of Effort or Different Way of Performance) and Consequences

Reduction or Addition of Positions (List)

$ Cost Decrease or Increase

Personnel	Nonpersonnel	Total

Revenue Impact

Exhibit A-4
Detailed Activity Decision Package: Branch Libraries

Page _____ of _____

No.	Activity Name	Department and/or Division
	Branch Libraries	Library

Reduction or Addition of Positions (List)

A. Alternative (Different Level of Effort or Different Way of Performance) and Consequences

Reduce hours of operation from 60 hrs./wk to 48 hrs.

—4 full-time positions

	Mon. & Wed.	1:00 P.M. to 9:00 P.M.
	Tues, Thurs, & Fri.	10:00 A.M. to 6:00 P.M.
	Sat.	9:00 A.M. to 5:00 P.M.

Consequence: Impact on the public is minimized with this schedule.

$ Cost Decrease or Increase

Personnel	Nonpersonnel	Total
—75,897	—900	—76,797

Revenue Impact
0

B. Alternative (Different Level of Effort or Different Way of Performance) and Consequences

Close Branch

—27 full-time positions

Consequence: Loss of neighborhood concept of service.

$ Cost Decrease or Increase

Personnel	Nonpersonnel	Total
—542,704	—68,161	—610,865

Revenue Impact
0

Exhibit A-5
Basic Needs Package for Department of Human Resources: Office of the Director   Sheet _1_ of _2_

No.	Activity Name	Position Titles	No. of Each Title	Percent of Positions at Peak	Personnel Cost
1	Administration				
	Description, purposes, objectives, or achievements	Director Admin. Officer Admin. Specialist	1 1 1 ―― 3	100 100 100 ――	86,333
	The office consists of three persons and maintains the overall direction of the Department and the direct operation of the Fenwick Center and the Madison Geriatric Center. The Administrative Officer for the two Centers doubles as the Administrative Aide to the Director, since there is no other support. The Director in addition to the relationships and responsibilities within the county is the Local Health Director and as such is directly responsible to the State Health Dept. and Regional Office and also maintains an interrelationship and responsibilities to the State Departments of Mental Health and Mental Retardation and Department of Welfare and its local and regional affiliates.	*State Reimbursement Director's Salary State Share Admin. Spec. and Fringes Nonpersonnel Costs	15,534 4,687 2,482 ―――― 22,703		*Nonpersonnel Cost* 4,513 *Total Cost* 90,846*
					Revenue: State, Federal, or Fees 22,720 *State Share*

A. Alternatives and Consequences—Either different ways of performing or different levels of effort.

There are no alternatives. The responsibilities and the hours worked in this office far exceed reasonable expectations.

	+ or (−) Personnel	+ or (−) Cost −1
	0	*Personnel* *Nonpersonnel*
B.	+ or (−) Personnel	*Personnel* *Nonpersonnel*

119

No.	Activity Name	Position Titles	No. of Each Title	Percent of Positions at Peak	Personnel Cost
2	Geriatric Activity Center (Madison)				115,663
	Description, purposes, objectives, or achievements	Supervisor	1	100	
		RN (PHN)	1	100	
		Mental Health Worker	1	100	*Nonpersonnel Cost*
		Social Worker	1	100	34,220
		Recreation Specialist	1	100	
		Clerk Typist II	1	100	
		Bus Driver/Custodian	2	100	*Total Cost*
		Geriatric Aide	9		149,883
					Revenue: State, Federal, or Fees
					50,000

To provide day care for the frail elderly, the mentally and physically handicapped, in order to improve and enhance their quality of life and their physical and mental condition and to maintain them in their place of residence in preference to an institution. A wing of Madison School is undergoing modification to remove architectural barriers and equip it for its new use. Fees will be charged on a sliding scale. In order to reduce the daily cost, it is essential that as many persons be served as possible, 60 persons must be served daily within 30 days of opening, i.e., 7/30/76. (A target of 75-80 persons could be served by including the 2 Geriatric Aides and 1 Bus Driver shown in Change Memo. Page 25, Volume II. Additional clients would reduce the daily cost and the additional fees would make the Center more self-supporting.) (See next sheet 2 of 2)

A. Alternatives and Consequences—Either different ways of performing or different levels.

				+ or (−) Personnel	+ or (−) Cost

This is a new program and one for which there is no model and no experience elsewhere. Revenue will be maximized. No alternative is proposed. Experience will dictate the appropriate level of staffing and adjustments will need to be made in order to serve more (or less) clients. Since persons will attend one or more days weekly, a potential 100-250 persons could be served with this level of staffing. Preference will be given to full-week clients whose responsible relative must work.

				+ or (−) Personnel	Personnel
B.					Nonpersonnel

Exhibit A-5 continued

No.	Activity Name	Position Titles	No. of Each Title	Percent of Positions at Peak	Personnel Cost
2a	Geriatric Activity Center Change Memorandum	Geriatric Aides (Home Health Aides)	2	100	30,404
		Bus Driver/Custodian	1	100	
	Description, purposes, objectives, or achievements				*Nonpersonnel Cost*
	The Fiscal 1977 Continuing Budget includes nine staff members for the Geriatric Activity Center as shown in preceding Number 2 Basic Needs Package-Detail. Fees are an essential part of the program and will be charged on a sliding scale. It is necessary that as many persons be served as possible to minimize the daily cost per client. To accomplish this, a minimum of 60 persons must be served daily as soon as possible after opening July 1, 1976. Space and facilities available in the Center are capable of accommodating 75-80 persons, but to achieve this target it is necessary to include 2 Geriatric Aides and 1 Bus Driver/Custodian shown in Change Memorandum, Page 25, Volume II of the budget. Additional clients would spread the costs over a greater number thereby reducing the daily cost and the added revenue would reduce the need for County support.				*Total Cost* 30,404
					Revenue: State, Federal, or Fees
					Est. Fees 30,000
A. *Alternatives and Consequences–Either different ways of performing or different levels of effort.*				+ or (−) Personnel	+ or (−) Cost −1
These positions are essential to achieve the goal of 75-80 clients daily thus maximizing revenues and making the Center more self-supporting. No alternative is proposed.					*Personnel*
					Nonpersonnel
B.				+ or (−) Personnel	*Personnel*
					Nonpersonnel

No.	Activity Name	Position Titles	No. of Each Title	Percent of Positions at Peak	Personnel Cost
	Description, purposes, objectives, or achievements				Nonpersonnel Cost
					Total Cost
					Revenue: State, Federal, or Fees

A. Alternatives and Consequences—Either different ways of performing or different levels.

+ or (−) Personnel	+ or (−) Cost
	Personnel
	Nonpersonnel

B.

+ or (−) Personnel	Personnel
	Nonpersonnel

Exhibit A-6
Detailed Activity Decision Package: Department of Human Resources   Page __2__ of __3__

No.	Activity Name	Department and/or Division	Type
1	Administrative Unit	Department of Human Resources Mental Health Services Division	[x] Basic Needs Activity for which an alternative level of effort suggests detailed analysis [ ] Activity is considered outside Basic Needs Category

Purpose/Objective

Purpose: To provide effective administrative support to the Division to assure the availability of services to the maximum number of Arlington residents possible, within available resources.

Description of (a) operations or actions (b) achievements or results, and/or (c) workload/performance measures at PRESENTLY BUDGETED LEVEL	Position Titles	No. of Each Title	Percent of Positions at Peak	Cost
(a) Operations: Plans and coordinates consultation and provision of direct services to high-risk groups. Plans and conducts training and staff development activities. Plans and coordinates the use and supervision of volunteers needed to expand the volume of patients served and the variety of services offered. Consults with other county agencies in the planning and coordination of services and develops and negotiates appropriate affiliation agreements and contracts as required by the State Department of Mental Health and Mental Retardation. Implements and supervises the procedures for the collection of appropriate fees. Coordinates the provision of administrative clerical support for the program units and conducts data collection and analysis and the preparation and submission of required reports. Assists in planning, implementing, and monitoring of management information and evaluation systems	Mental Health Division Director	1	All 100%	*Personnel* 157,675
	Mental Health Planner-Administrator	1		
	Clerical Support Supervisor	1		
	*Psychiatric Social Worker	1		
	Vol. Svcs. Coord.	1		*Nonpersonnel* 14,677
	*Admin. Spec.	2		
	Acct. Clk.	1		
	Services Clk.	1		
	Services Clk. (132)	1		*Total* 172,352
	Clk. Typists (132)	2		
	Custodial Worker	1		
				Revenue: State, Federal, or Fees state: 58,217
	*1 Psychiatric Social Worker is assigned to the Geriatric Services Unit, and 1 Administrative Specialist is assigned to the Interdivisional Services Teams			*Percent of Department Budget* 1.25%

No.	Activity Name	Department and/or Division
1	Administrative Unit	Department of Human Resources Mental Health Services Division

A. Alternative (Different Level of Effort or Different Way of Performance) and Consequences

Reduction or Addition of Positions (List)
Eliminate One Volunteer Services Coordinator –1.

$ Cost Decrease or Increase			
Personnel	Nonpersonnel	Total	Revenue Impact
–11,871	–250	–12,121	*See below

Alternative: To eliminate the Volunteer Services Coordinator and decrease unclassified services by $250. The Volunteer Services Coordinator's role was to design volunteer services to supplement existing staff resources.

Consequences: The support functions necessary to adequately maintain a functional unit in which volunteers can be trained and supervised would have to be continued by professionally trained staff. This would result in:

(a) Fewer persons being treated or served directly. This would amount to 7.25 fewer persons per therapist being served as 25% of professional time is now planned for necessary administrative work and emergency coverage.

(b) The vital and necessary public role needed by the Mental Health Division would be affected adversely. Community education projects could not be undertaken and the recruitment and training of new volunteers would not be possible.

(c) Planned volunteer support programs for previously hospitalized chronically ill patients will not be able to be effected. This is particularly critical now since the State's deinstitutionalization policy is returning an increased number of patients of limited functioning to the community.

B. Alternative (Different Level of Effort or Different Way of Performance) and Consequences

Reduction or Addition of Positions (List)

$ Cost Decrease or Increase			
Personnel	Nonpersonnel	Total	Revenue Impact

*Although the Mental Health Division's programs are state grant-funded, there would be no reduction of state funds with the total magnitude of possible program reductions included in the Decision Packages for Mental Health. However, if program reductions were to exceed approximately $50,000, Arlington could lose revenue.

124

Exhibit A-7
Detailed Activity Decision Package: Department of Human Resources　　　　Page __3__ of __3__

No.	Activity Name	Department and/or Division	Reduction or Addition of Positions (List)
1	School Health Services Division	Department of Human Resources	Eliminate 4 positions. Cut 1 nurse position by attrition. Lay off 1 nurse and 2 school health aides. Cut audiometrists' time by 1/9.

A. Alternative (Different Level of Effort or Different Way of Performance) and Consequences

10% budget cut.

Consequences:

1. Reassign the 4 schools involved with nursing reduction (Williamsburg Junior High—census 845; Jamestown Elementary—521; Key Elementary—567; Tuckahoe Elementary—438; total census 2,371) which:

   (a) Increases pupil/nurse ratios above the present level of 1:1200, which is already higher than the 1:1000 recommended by the American School Health Association.

   (b) Causes unequal assignments among remaining staff due to significant differences in school sizes.

   (c) Reduces efficiency of nurses as they cover more buildings over wider geographic area.

   (d) Reduces school nursing service to schools from 140 days/week to 120 days/week which is a 15% reduction of time.

   (e) Eliminates some specific services, e.g., athletic clearances—3,982 students; work permit physical examinations—892; services to medically indigent, nonmedicaid—341.

2. Eliminates all School Health Aide assistance to elementary schools (26 buildings with total census of 10,426). Eliminates the one day/week School Health Aide assistance to the Medicaid program for required paper work.

3. Reduces audiometrists' time by discontinuing part of hearing testing programs, such as discontinuing testing in the Senior High schools.

4. Violates the "Criteria for Maintaining the Present Levels of School Health Service" as agreed upon by the School Board and County Board in July 1973—see attachment.

$ Cost Decrease or Increase

Personnel	Nonpersonnel	Total
−$49,708.	−$160 −$294 −$ 45 −$499.	−$50,207
		Revenue Impact

B. Alternative (Different Level of Effort or Different Way of Performance) and Consequences

20% budget cut.

Consequences:

1. Reassign the 10 schools (8 elementary and 2 junior high schools) which:
   (a) Increases nurse/pupil ratios from 1:1200 as noted in (A) above.
   (b) Causes unequal assignments among staff with the nurse/pupil ratios ranging as widely as 1:1400 to 1:2000. Smaller elementary schools which now have one nursing day/week would see a nurse, at best, only one day every 2 weeks. Junior high schools, which now have a nurse 3 days/week will be reduced to 2 days/week. All senior high schools which now have a nurse 5 days/week will be reduced to 4 days/week.
   (c) Reduces further the efficiency of nurses as their services become more fragmented.
   (d) Reduces nursing service to schools from 140 days/week to 100 days/week which is a 29% reduction of time.
   (e) Eliminates more services than those noted above in (A), e.g., discontinues all health education activities; discontinues all home visiting; discontinues retesting students who fail vision screening before referral.
2. Reduces School Health Aide assistance to all 10 secondary schools by 1 day/week each, as well as eliminating aide assignments as noted in (A) above.
3. Reduces audiometrists time as in (A) above.
4. Violates the "Criteria for Maintaining the Present Levels of School Health Service" as agreed by the School Board and County Board in July 1973—see attachment.

Reduction or Addition of Positions (List)

Eliminate 8 positions.

Cut 1 nurse position by attrition.

Lay off 3 nurses and 4 school health aides.

Cut audiometrists' time by 1/9.

$ Cost Decrease or Increase

Personnel	Nonpersonnel	Total
−$97,526.	−$480 −$862 −$ 45 −$1,387.	−$98,913
		Revenue Impact

126

Exhibit A-8
Detailed Activity Decision Package: Department of Human Resources

Page 7c of 7

No.	Activity Name	Department and/or Division
11	Assistances and Purchased Services Foster Care	Department of Human Resources Social Services Division

A. Alternative (Different Level of Effort or Different Way of Performance) and Consequences

Foster Care funds are utilized to provide maintenance and services for children who are in the custody of the Board of Public Welfare. Alternative living arrangements range from traditional foster homes to highly specialized residential treatment centers for the emotionally disturbed or developmentally disabled.

From a current total of 73 children in all types of institutional placements, a projected net increase of 12 is expected to raise the number of children in institutional care to a total of 85 as of July 1, 1976. A reduction in local funds for the foster care program can be accomplished by restricting placements of children in institutional care to the July 1, 1976 level. This will allow the Division to remain within the continuing budget forecast for fiscal year 1977. (Further details are provided in Change Memorandum p. 36 and 37 Proposed Budget, Vol. 2.) In addition, maximum use of Title XX funds will have to be made giving preference to foster care services over other services identified as priorities by the County Board; transportation for Title XX eligibles, Adult Day Care, and Child Care.

Consequences:

1. The Courts will have to seek other alternatives for children not able to remain in their own homes; such as, commitment to the State Department of Corrections.
2. An increased demand for supervision of children by staff of the Juvenile Court and the Social Services Division already working with caseloads which surpass the maximum standard established by the State.

Reduction or Addition of Positions (List)

None

	$ Cost Decrease or Increase		
	Personnel	Nonpersonnel	Total
	None	–$159,480	–$159,480
			Revenue Impact
			–$79,740

No.	Activity Name	Department and/or Division	Reduction or Addition of Positions (List)

B. Alternative (Different Level of Effort or Different Way of Performance) and Consequences

$ Cost Decrease or Increase			
Personnel	Nonpersonnel	Total	
			Revenue Impact

Exhibit A-9

Detailed Activity Decision Package: Department of Property Management

Page _____ of _____

No.	Activity Name	Department and/or Division
5	Truck	Equipment Division 09.1066

A. Alternative (Different Level of Effort or Different Way of Performance) and Consequences

Alternative is to freeze Auto Mechanic I, Welder and Auto Mechanic Crew Leader positions in FY 77. A Public Service Worker I position will become vacant in August 1976 with the retirement of the incumbent. This position would be frozen. This general reduction is feasible if the workload decreases with anticipation that the line departments will be cutting programs. It is also important that replacement of the equipment continues or the fleet age will work against us by making us rely on older equipment to perform those jobs and programs which are retained in FY 77.

Some welding services will be done by an outside contractor. The shop welders not only work on our automotive equipment but do work for the other departments, i.e., fabricating manhole covers, cutting steel forms, etc. Mechanics will have to pick up more of their own parts and clean up their work areas.

Reduction or Addition of Positions (List)

Auto Mech Crew Leader–freeze position
Auto Mech I–freeze position
Welder–freeze position
Public Service Worker I–freeze

$ Cost Decrease or Increase

Personnel	Nonpersonnel	Total
(45,000)	(10,000)	(55,000)
		Revenue Impact
		(55,000)

B. Alternative (Different Level of Effort or Different Way of Performance) and Consequences

Reduction or Addition of Positions (List)

$ Cost Decrease or Increase

Personnel	Nonpersonnel	Total
		Revenue Impact

Appendix B:
Washington Metropolitan Area Transit Authority Fiscal Year 1978 Decision Packages

This appendix reproduces selected portions of the decision packages considered by the METRO Transit Authority Budget Committee in its work on the fiscal year 1978 budget and the budget decisions made by the committee. Decision packages are presented for offices of secretary-treasurer, data processing, metrorail operations, systems, and planning, and the plant maintenance department. Budget committee decisions on the plant maintenance department are presented in the committee's minutes of November 8, 1976.

Exhibit B-1

Washington Metropolitan Area Transit Authority Effect of 15 Percent Reduction to FY 1978 Budget Estimates: Secretary-Treasurer Percent

Office of Secretary-Treasurer

	FY 1978 Estimate	FY 1978 Revised	Change	Percent Change
Number of Positions (year-end)	111	98	(13)	(11.7)
Number of Man-Years	110.75	97.75	(13)	(11.7)
Personnel Costs	$2,099,500	$2,800,380	$299,120	(14.3)
Nonpersonnel Costs (List reductions to major items)	$ 860,800	$ 711,075	$149,725	(17.4)

Salaries reduced by $256,209.

Fringe benefits reduced by $42,911.

Materials and Supplies reduced by $86,725.

Services—Professional and Technical reduced by $36,000.

Services—Dues and Subscriptions reduced by $14,000.

Services—Travel and Meetings reduced by $13,000.

Total Costs	$2,960,300	$2,511,455	$448,845	(15.2)

Effect on FY 1978 Programs, Functions, and Service as a Result of Reductions

1. The elimination of the following positions in Fiscal 1978:

1 Supervision Station Collection	$ 19,018
1 Assistant Supervisor Coin Room	16,907
1 Financial Assistant	13,130
10 Revenue Attendants	125,480
1 Clerk Typist	10,314

Reductions of salary expense are made possible by reducing the service of the AFCS equipment from daily to every other day. SECT estimates that ½ the capacity or $275,000 would remain uncollected nightly. This would increase the Authoritiy's exposure to theft. Another point to consider is the accuracy of the PLAN estimates of ridership. Should they continue to be understated (PLAN estimated average daily ridership at 8500—actual ridership is 20,000) and should a sheep syndrome (patrons lining up in front of one machine) develop, the capacities of the vending machines may not be adequate. Sheep syndrome occurs regularly at BART and has occurred at our Rhode Island Avenue Station parking token vendor. The cost to SURE to reduce this exposure has not been addressed. Should the Authority find itself in a borrowing situation, like that of last year, the cost of money could become another factor in evaluating this approach.

2. Benefits on the positions cut above
3. Prohibit the use of currency in the bus farebox
4. The elimination of uniforms for both the coin room and station collections crews. Uniforms for these employees were to be furnished in response to requests from SURE and from the employees.
5. The packaging of tokens of 50 rather than envelopes of 10. Adoption of this procedure

Exhibit B-1 (cont.)

would result in a savings to SECT but would affect MARK. Further it may adversely affect the distributions of tokens to the public in that consignee may not wish to handle unpackaged tokens, nor will the public be prepared to make the large ($20.00) outlay for one whole tube of tokens without some discount offered.

6. Office supply requirements are also reduced due to deletions of personnel.
7. Eliminating the use of paper tickets in the bus farebox. Note: (1) Additional tokens would be required at a one time cost of $40,000; (2) the cost of ticket printing is born by TRAN.
8. Reduce the scope of the independent audit by 20 percent.
9. Resigning from APTA and eliminating the Authority's participation at out of town APTA conferences.
10. Eliminate the Airlie Conference as presently constituted.

Exhibit B-2
Washington Metropolitan Area Transit Authority Effect of 15 Percent Reduction to FY 1978 Budget Estimates: Data Processing

Office of Data Processing

	FY 1978 Estimate	FY 1978 Revised	Change	Percent Change
Number of Positions (year-end)	83	81	(2)	(2.4)
Number of Man-Years	80	78.5	(1.5)	(1.9)
Personnel Costs	$1,576,400	$1,545,642	$ (30,758)	(2)
Nonpersonnel Costs (List reductions to major items)	$3,428,300	$2,690,300	$(738,000)	(21.5)

Professional and Technical Services reduced by $738,000.

| Total Costs | $5,004,700 | $4,235,942 | $ 768,758 | (15.4) |

Effect on FY 1978 Programs, Functions, and Service as a Result of Reductions

The reduction in Professional and Technical Services of $738,000 reflects delays in the implementation phase of the Rail Maintenance System to FY 1979 ($648,000) and of the Bus Scheduling System to the second quarter of FY 1979 ($90,000). Due to the complexities of these systems and the coordinated effort required by several offices and departments, delay of the implementation phase until FY 1979 is not unrealistic and will not impair program.

The deletion of 2 positions (one Computer Operator (TA-8) and one Data Base Analyst (TA-11), both requested in FY 1979, can be accomplished due to delays in implementing the Rail Maintenance System and Bus Scheduling System. These two positions were programmed for support in this area but will not be required until FY 1979.

Exhibit B-3

Washington Metropolitan Area Transit Authority Effect of 15 Percent Reduction to FY 1978 Budget Estimates: Metrorail Operations

Metrorail Operations

	FY 1978 Estimate	FY 1978 Revised	Change	Percent Change
Number of Positions (year-end)				
Number of Man-Years				
Personnel Costs	$6,675,900	$5,781,400	$894,500	13.4
Nonpersonnel Costs	$ 361,800	$ 291,600	$ 70,200	16

There will be a decrease in the number of Automatic Fare Collections Cards purchased.

	FY 1978 Estimate	FY 1978 Revised	Change	Percent Change
Total Costs	$7,037,700	$6,073,000	$964,700	13.7

Effect on FY 1978 Programs, Functions, and Service as a Result of Reductions

The following station entrances and kiosks will be closed, resulting in great inconvenience to passengers. This will result in a reduction of 26 station attendants for a saving of $513,800.

	Scheduled	Revised	Reduction
DuPont Circle	2	1	1
Farragut North	3	2	1
METRO Center	4	3	1
Gallery Place	2	1	1
Judiciary Square	2	1	1
Farragut West	2	1	1
McPherson Square	2	1	1
Smithsonian	2	1	1
L'Enfant Plaza	3	2	1
	22	13	9

The following cuts in train service will affect all lines, resulting in catastrophic overcrowding and safety conditions. This will result in a reduction of 17 train operators for a saving of $353,600.

	Rush Hour Headway	(Base) (Headway)	No. of Trains per Rush Hour	No. of Cars per Rush Hour	Passenger Capacity Comfort Load
Scheduled	5 Min.	(10)	24-6 car	144	25,200
Revised	10 Min.	(15)	12-8 car	96	16,800

There will be a decrease of two secretaries scheduled for the Division Superintendent and Operations Control Center Offices. This will result in a saving of $27,100.

It is recommended that in lieu of the above reductions the following 5.6 percent reduction be accepted—14-hour, 5-day operation continue during the Phase III operation resulting in the following saving in training cost, man-years, and end strength occurring in FY 1978.

End Strength	Man-Years	$$
171	19.7	$394,600

Exhibit B-4

Washington Metropolitan Area Transit Authority Effect of 15 Percent Reduction to FY 1978 Budget Estimates: Systems

Systems

	FY 1978 Estimate	FY 1978 Revised	Change	Percent Change
Number of Positions (year-end)				
Number of Man-Years				
Personnel Costs	$7,635,500	$6,303,646	$1,331,854	17.4%
Nonpersonnel Costs (List reductions to major items)	$9,512,100	$8,085,285	$1,426,815	15%
Propulsion Power	2,479,200	2,107,320	371,880	15%
Unit Power (AC)	5,770,900	4,905,265	865,635	15%
Spare Parts and Material	941,400	800,190	141,210	15%
Total Costs	$17,147,600	$14,388,931	$2,758,669	16%

Effect on FY 1978 Programs, Functions, and Service as a Result of Reductions

Personnel Costs
In order to achieve a 15% reduction in costs, TA man-years reduced from 87.00 to 72.5 and union man-years reduced from 245.5 to 202, yielding a combined man-year savings of 58.0 man-years. This will mean a slower response time to system problems and some deferred maintenance to non-safety-critical equipments.

The manpower cuts represent reductions in non-safety-critical areas of Automatic Fare Collection, bus radio systems, and central control computer maintenance. These tasks are now programs which are first addressed in the FY 78 budget. Staff reductions will lengthen planned response time and require the establishment of deferred maintenance schedules in non-safety related areas.

Non-Personnel Costs
The nonpersonnel costs are predominantly electrical operating costs for both Traction and Station Power. Traction power is a linear function of car miles. Using an estimated 10.6 KWH per car mile, an 8-car train represents 84 KWH per mile of operation. Using an estimated 0.5 per KWK this equals $4.20. The 15% reduction in Traction power budget fund represents $371,880 or 708,342 car miles.

The reduction of station electrical budget will require a program of selective load sheding and power system management. To accomplish this goal a concerted program reducing air conditioning, escalator operation, and operation from station essential buses must be practiced to establish the threshold levels which the Authority can live with. Once this standard is established, the actual energy conservation savings may be calculated.

Spare parts and material—A reduction of 15% in draw down of spare parts from the store room would mean that *some* of the plant in place would not be repaired. We would repair safety-critical equipments.

Exhibit B-5

Washington Metropolitan Area Transit Authority Effect of 15 Percent Reduction to FY 1978 Budget Estimates: Planning

Office of Planning

	FY 1978 Estimate	FY 1978 Revised	Change	Percent Change
Number of Positions (year-end)	49	44	(5)	(10.2)
Number of Man-Years	48.75	44.00	(4.75)	(9.7)
Personnel Costs	$1,441,400	$1,361,891	$ (79,509)	(5.5)
Nonpersonnel Costs (List reductions to major items)	$ 591,700	$ 367,200	$(224,500)	(37.9)
Professional and Technical Services				
a. Metrobus-Metrorail Ridership Survey		$ 52,500		
b. Data Processing Services		35,000		
c. Economic Route Analysis		100,000		
Total		$ 187,500		
Travel and Meetings		2,000		
Materials and Supplies		3,000		
Printing and Reproduction		27,000		
Temporary Help		5,000		
Total		$ 224,500		
Total Costs	$2,033,100	$1,729,091	$(304,009)	(15.0)

Effect on FY 1978 Programs, Functions, and Service as a Result of Reductions

Transportation Economist (TA-8)—Elimination of this additional position for FY 1978 will hinder the development of input for the Metrobus and Metrorail operating subsidies for current fiscal year requirements. This will, in turn, impact upon the ability of PLNG to respond in a timely fashion to requests from the local jurisdictions on changes in subsidy level due to service changes. In addition, the planned effort on economic route analysis will be reduced.

Administrative Aide (TA-8)—Elimination of this additional position for FY 1978 will require that key staff personnel devote time to administrative details on a daily basis, delaying the solution of more important problems.

Additional Staff Reductions
Clerk-Typist (TA-5)—Elimination of this existing position will require reassignment of functions now performed by the Director's Office among the various sections and shifting secretarial and typing skills to meet the critical demands even more than is now necessary. PLNG's response to routine citizens' inquiries and requests for information will be substantially slowed with the loss of this position.

Position (TA-8), Bus Shelter Program—No particular individual is assigned to this program. Various individuals, with an average grade of 8, expend about one man-year on this program. Should the budget require the elimination of the Bus Shelter Program, PLNG will accomplish the savings through reorganization and eliminate one existing position.

Exhibit B-5 (cont.)

Position (TA-8)—The Capital Bus Stop and Replacement Program initiated by the Board is about 1/3 completed. One person is required full-time for this program. It is anticipated that the new capital program will be completed during FY 1979. Subsequent to that program, the maintenance of this useful information aide will require the services of one person due to service changes, detours, reroutings, and service additions and deletions.

Professional and Technical Services

Metrobus-Metrorail Ridership Survey: The reduction in survey costs of $52,500 (15%) reflects a reduced collection of data for the allocation of revenues to the various jurisdictions. In addition, special requests from the local jurisdictions on the affects of charges in the formulae will have to be done by the jurisdictions in lieu of the Authority staff. $52,500

Data Processing Services: This amount was budgeted for outside data processing services to provide data on the bus-rail deficit allocation formulas and provide forecast for revenues, costs, and patronage. The elimination of this cost will result in delays in providing this type information on request, unless such work can be provided inhouse by Data Processing. $35,000

Economic Route Analysis: This cost was budgeted to analyze individual Metrobus routes to determine their true cost effectiveness. During FY 1977, WMATA, together with UMTA/APTA, was to develop techniques for the economic evaluation. Due to recent delays by UMTA in the development of the program, it is unlikely that the program will be completed for WMATA's use in FY 1978 and, therefore, can be eliminated from the FY 1978 budget. $100,000

Travel and Meetings

$2,000

Most of PLNG expenditures for this item are programmed for public hearings, public forums, and various local jurisdictional meetings. PLNG cannot control the number of meetings staff will be required to attend, but it has considerably reduced the number of persons attending public hearings.

Printing and Reproduction

$27,000

The reduction in printing and reproduction costs represents a reduction in the number of public hearing documents printed for distribution to the public and local jurisdictions. The staff proposes that for future public hearings, public hearing documents be made available at all public libraries for review by the public and that no copies be sent to individuals and organizations. In addition, reports submitted to the Board for action will not be resubmitted when action is deferred.

Temporary Help

$5,000

Reduce temporary help by $5,000. This cost was budgeted to assist PLNG in the development, implementation, and evaluation of Metrobus service during implementation of Metrorail Phase II, IIA, and III; also, to assist PLNG staff in making Metrobus service adjustments to meet ridership demands.

Exhibit B-6

Washington Metropolitan Area Transit Authority Effect of 15 Percent Reduction to FY 1978 Budget Estimates: Plant Maintenance

Plant Maintenance (Total)

	FY 1978 Estimate	FY 1978 Revised	Change	Percent Change
Number of Positions (year-end)	341	297	44	13
Number of Man Years	313.25	252.55	60.70	20
Personnel Costs	$6,789,700	$5,576,650	$1,213,050	18
Nonpersonnel Costs (List reductions to major items)	$2,648,200	$2,440,500	$ 207,700	8
Services Prof. & Tech.	30,000	25,500	4,500	15%
Services Temporary Help	10,000	8,500	1,500	15%
Services Contract.	548,000	465,800	82,200	15%
Services Custodial	50,000	42,500	7,500	15%
Services Utilities	900,000	900,000	–	–
Services Dues	200	200	–	–
Services Travel	10,000	8,500	1,500	15%
Services Other	35,000	29,750	5,250	15%
Materials Fuel	2,000	1,700	300	15%
Materials Tires	13,000	11,050	1,950	15%
Materials Other	1,018,000	918,000	100,000	10%
Leases Property	12,000	12,000	–	–
Leases Vehicles	10,000	8,500	1,500	15%
Leases Equipment	10,000	8,500	1,500	15%
Total Costs	$9,437,900	$8,017,150	$1,420,750	16%

Effect on FY 1978 Programs, Functions, and Service as a Result of Reductions

1. Reduction in Contract Services will require cancelling or postponing needed repairs to roofs, parking lots, fences, etc.
2. Any reduction in Utilities account, would reduce below "bare bones."
3. Reduction in Travel will result from delay of bringing personnel aboard for training, i.e., reducing number of people available to be trained.
4. Reduction in Materials account could mean we would delay repairs or replacement of parts or equipment.
5. Property lease is a fixed cost of a 5-year lease.

Exhibit B-7
Washington Metropolitan Area Transit Authority Effect of 15 Percent Reduction to FY 1978 Budget Estimates: Plant Maintenance

Plant Maintenance (Bus)

	FY 1978 Estimate	FY 1978 Revised	Change	Percent Change
Number of Positions (year-end)	116.0	97.0	19	16.
Number of Man Years	110.57	96.32	14.25	13.0
Personnel Costs	$2,389,700	$2,138,350	$251,350	10.5
Nonpersonnel Costs (List reductions to major items)	$	$	$	
Total Costs	$	$	$	

Effect on FY 1978 Programs, Functions, and Service as a Result of Reductions

1. Increase overtime $40,000 to provide for emergency coverage.
2. Reduce bus shelter cleaning from once per week to once per 2 weeks. Loop cleaning reduce to once per day. — −6 Loop Attendants
3. Reduce Landscape Maintenance from once per 6 days to once per 8 days. — −1 Landscape/Laborer
4. Reduce supervision for custodial. — −1 Supervisor
5. Present response schedule for shelters is 75 days for repairs. Addition of 2 people was to bring response time back to 30 days. Reduce 2 people and return to 75 day repair time. — −1 Mechanic, −1 Helper
6. Presently have 2nd shift of 9 people. Reduce 1 Plumber, 1 Carpenter, and 1 Electrician. Eliminate 2nd shift and return to 1 shift. — −3 Mechanics
7. Addition of 4 Mechanics and 1 Helper was to establish a preventive maintenance program in garages. Eliminate and return to program of when it breaks down, fix it or replace it. — −4 Mechanics, −1 Helper
8. Addition of 1 Clerk and 1 Timekeeper (1/2 Bus and 1/2 Rail) was to reduce Supervisors' time in preparing and recording time cards, time sheets, and purchase requisitions. — −1/2 Clerk, −1/2 Timekeeper

Exhibit B-8

Washington Metropolitan Area Transit Authority Effect of 15 Percent Reduction to FY 1978 Budget Estimates: Plant Maintenance

Plant Maintenance (Rail)

	FY 1978 Estimate	FY 1978 Revised	Change	Percent Change
Number of Positions (year-end)	225	200	25	12
Number of Man Years	202.68	156.23	46.45	23
Personnel Costs	$4,400,00	$3,438,300	$961,700	22
Nonpersonnel Costs (List reductions to major items)	$	$	$	—
Total Costs	$	$	$	—

Effect on FY 1978 Programs, Functions, and Service as a Result of Reductions

1. Reduce present cleaning and trash removal cycle in Rail Stations of 1/2 man per station to 1/3 man per station per shift. — −12 Janitors
2. Eliminate emergency crews, 3 shifts × 7 days, and respond with overtime. — −11 Mechanics
3. Increase overtime $57,060 to provide for emergency coverage. — −2 Supervisors
4. Delay addition of 3 Track Supervisors until 4th quarter. Result in increased risk of accidents in Track Maintenance tasks. — −1 1/2 Man Years
5. Delay addition of 29 Union employees to 20 weeks prior to end of FY 78. — −10 1/2 Man Years
6. Delay 28 Union people to 10 weeks prior to end of FY 78. Note: 5 and 6 above will result in delay of acceptance of 11 rail stations, subcontract maintenance on capital program at a substantially higher cost. — −15 1/2 Man Years
7. Addition of 1 Clerk and 1 Timekeeper (1/2 Bus and 1/2 Rail) was to reduce Supervisors' time in preparing and recording time sheets and purchase requisitions. Continue present method with Supervisors. — −1/2 Clerk −1/2 Timekeeper

Exhibit B-9
Board Budget Committee, November 8, 1976

Decisions/Policy

Plant Maintenance

The Plant Maintenance Department was reviewed and reductions were made by reducing cleaning standards for bus shelters and rail stations, delaying response time for repair of bus shelters, providing emergency repairs on overtime basis rather than staffing emergency crews, reductions in preventive maintenance programs, reducing clerical support, and eliminating expanded service concurrent with Phase III Rail operations. A summary of these reductions is as follows:

2	TA-10 Supervisor of Building Maintenance	$ 32,100
3	TA-10 Track and Way Supervisor	48,200
1	TA-9 Assistant Shift Sup–Custodial	14,300
1	TA-5 Clerk Typist	8,700
1	TA-5 Timekeeper	8,700
6	Union Mechanic AA	101,800
8	Union Mechanic A	131,000
3	Union Mechanic B	48,300
3	Union Helper	44,800
12	Union Janitors	191,300
4	Union Loop Attendant	48,300
6	Union Track Inspector	54,400
50	Total Personnel Costs Reduction	$731,900
	Reduce Professional & Technical	3,000
	Reduce Temporary Help	1,500
	Reduce Contract Maintenance	58,800
	Reduce Custodial	6,500
	Reduce Travel	1,000
	Reduce Services–Other	4,500
	Reduce Materials & Supplies–Fuel	200
	Reduce Materials & Supplies–Tires	1,000
	Reduce Materials & Supplies–Other	81,500
	Reduce Leases–Vehicles	1,000
	Reduce Leases–Equipment	1,000
	Total Nonpersonnel Cost Reduction	$160,000
	Total Reduction	$891,900

Appendix C:
Arlington County Fiscal
Year 1978 Proposed
Budget

This appendix reproduces selected portions of Arlington County's proposed budget for fiscal year 1978: the budget summary and portions of the budget presentations for the office of consumer affairs, the police department, nondepartmental, and the social services division.

Exhibit C-1
Arlington County Budget Summary, Fiscal Year 1978

PAGE	AGENCY	FISCAL YEAR 1977 APPROVED PROGRAM LEVEL			FISCAL YEAR 1978 RECOMMENDED PROGRAM LEVEL			FISCAL YEAR 1978 FUNDING OPTIONS — REDUCED PROGRAM LEVEL			FISCAL YEAR 1978 FUNDING OPTIONS — INCREASED PROGRAM LEVEL		
		Costs	Revenues	Net General Fund	Costs	Revenues	Net General Fund	Costs	Revenues	Net General Fund	Costs	Revenues	Net General Fund
	GENERAL FUND:												
3	01.1010 County Board	156,769		156,769	152,951		152,951				9,120		9,120
5	01.1020 County Manager	380,451	120,232	260,219	352,586	105,500	247,086				18,000		18,000
11	01.1030 Management Systems and Budget	1,296,608	599,668	696,940	1,404,800	796,930	607,870				59,704	59,704	59,704
19	01.1040 Extension Service, VPI	90,493	9,806	80,687	94,338	10,100	84,238				6,172		6,172
25	01.1060 Property Management	1,655,291	390,481	1,264,810	1,687,884	370,912	1,316,972	(8,218)		(8,218)			
35	01.1070 Personnel	736,611	90,582	646,029	822,819	101,000	721,819	(3,076)		(3,076)	11,242		11,242
45	01.1080 County Attorney	179,786		179,786	196,305		196,305	(39,854)		(39,854)	32,000		32,000
47	01.1110 Circuit Court	178,701		178,701	182,210		182,210	(45,785)		(45,785)			
49	01.1130 District Court	330,800		330,800	305,721		305,721						
53	01.1160 Juvenile and Domestic Relations District Court	936,220	441,558	494,662	911,027	407,377	503,650				26,617	8,699	17,938
59	01.1180 County Clerk	220,668	6,155	214,513	237,901	6,622	231,279						
63	01.1310 Commonwealth's Attorney	243,520	77,300	166,220	269,332	94,056	175,276						
67	01.1320 Alcohol Safety Action Program	263,647	263,647		252,558	231,837	20,721	(20,721)		(20,721)			
71	01.1410 Sheriff and Jail	1,378,055	764,078	566,977	1,445,700	869,164	576,536						
77	01.1610 Commissioner of the Revenue	879,830	275,695	604,135	880,790	290,223	590,567				23,610	5,471	18,139
93	01.1620 Real Estate Assessments	361,075		361,075	385,579		385,579				44,900		44,900
87	01.1630 Reassessment Commission							(11,240)		(11,240)			
89	01.1710 Treasurer	860,088	262,010	578,058	851,553	275,000	576,553		18,000	(18,000)	10,176	3,176	7,000
95	01.1810 Electoral Board	140,257	16,200	124,057	134,463	17,010	117,453				9,360		9,160
95	01.1910 Consumer Affairs	113,875		113,875	110,577		110,577				14,499		14,499
105	01.2020 Police	8,654,767	251,608	8,403,159	9,432,038	296,889	9,135,149	(15,176)		(15,176)	19,240		19,240
115	01.2030 Fire	6,131,206	312,692	5,818,514	6,393,247	327,400	6,065,847	(1,000,057)		(1,000,057)	11,250	11,250	-0-
123	01.2050 Inspection	899,879	532,921	366,958	922,135	606,858	315,277	(139,082)		(139,082)	57,607		57,607
129	01.3010 Utilities	3,155,537	1,735,821	1,419,716	3,082,646	1,678,046	1,384,600	(18,675)		(18,675)	-0-		-0-
137	01.3040 Transportation	4,176,756	381,099	3,795,657	4,229,631	337,624	3,892,007	(50,647)	634,500	(685,147)	139,697	59,962	79,735
155	01.4010 Human Resources	2,379,272	200,362	2,178,910	4,310,596	2,169,932	2,140,664	(114,851)		(114,851)	127,845	48,046	79,799
175	01.5010 Library	2,013,647	379,260	1,634,387	2,130,585	210,000	1,920,585	(76,172)	(10,596)	(65,576)	11,962		11,962
187	01.6010 Environmental Affairs	5,409,097	1,043,137	4,365,960	5,660,711	1,197,146	4,463,565	(163,788)	(12,945)	(163,788)	143,563	5,000	138,563
219	01.7010 Non-Departmental	2,417,384		2,417,384	11,694,839		11,694,839	(42,000)		(42,000)			
223	01.8010 Debt Service	12,365,749		12,365,249	3,908,100		3,908,100						
225	01.8610 Regional Contributions	557,017		557,017	546,678		546,678						
227	01.8620 Metro	1,078,000		1,028,000	5,100,000	5,100,000	5,100,000						
	OTHER OPERATING FUNDS:												
231	02.4010 Virginia Public Assistance Fund	9,689,578	7,184,953	2,504,625	7,096,391	4,457,833	2,638,558	(188,621)	(70,501)	(118,120)	378,648	170,359	208,289
245	03.3010 Utilities Fund	10,228,567	10,228,567		10,098,362	10,098,162					1,564,000	1,564,000	1,564,000
253	04.4090 Federal Revenue Sharing Fund	352,396		352,396	50,922	43,003	7,919						
259	05.2017 Dog Tax Fund	6,051	6,051		6,051								
259	06.4028 Mental Health Services Board Fund	967,982	900,375	67,607	927,957	770,948	156,999	(8,314)	(603)	(7,711)			
265	08.1064 Central Stores Fund	83,060	83,060		88,208		88,208						
267	09.1060 Automotive Equipment Fund	2,174,076	2,101,500	72,576	1,304,676	2,320,696	(16,020)				141,502	112,330	29,172
273	10.3620 NVTC Fund	701,728		701,728	432,000		432,000						

Exhibit C-2
Arlington County Budget: Office of Consumer Affairs Organization Chart, FY 1978

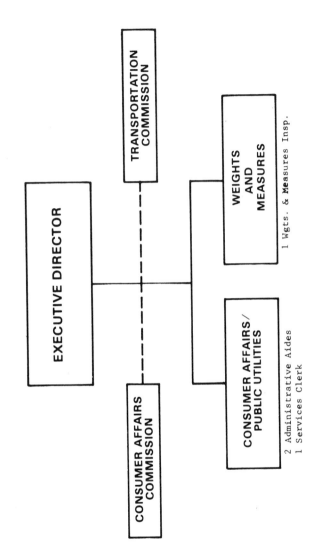

Exhibit C-3

Arlington County Budget: Consumer Affairs Summary, FY 1978

PAGE	ACTIVITY DESCRIPTION	FISCAL YEAR 1977			FISCAL YEAR 1978 FUNDING OPTIONS								
		APPROVED PROGRAM LEVEL			RECOMMENDED PROGRAM LEVEL			REDUCED PROGRAM LEVEL			INCREASED PROGRAM LEVEL		
		Costs	Revenues	Net General Fund	Costs	Revenues	Net General Fund	Costs	Revenues	Net General Fund	Costs	Revenues	Net General Fund
	OFFICE OF CONSUMER AFFAIRS												
100	PUBLIC UTILITIES	9,032		9,032	5,190		5,190						
100	CONSUMER AFFAIRS	81,189		81,189	84,369		84,369						
100 101	CABLE TELEVISION - Add an Administrative Aide	5,892		5,892	5,070		5,070				14,499		14,499
101 101	WEIGHTS AND MEASURES - Eliminate Weights and Measures inspector position	13,159		13,159	11,137		11,137	(15,176)		(15,176)			
103	TAXICAB REGULATION	4,604		4,604	4,812		4,812						
	TOTAL	113,875		113,875	110,577		110,577	(15,176)		(15,176)	14,499		14,499

Exhibit C-4
Arlington County Budget: Consumer Affairs, FY 1978

228

I N C R E A S E

ALTERNATIVE 1 DESCRIBE CHANGE, IMPACT AND CONSEQUENCES This alternative would add one Administrative Aide to increase cable television monitoring and activity consonant with the cable television certificate holder's increased construction planning, and cablecasting planning. Likely commitment of county resources for oversight was given as partial justification for the granting by FCC of the county's request for approval of the 4% gross receipts tax which was in excess of the FCC's maximum allowable 3% of subscriber revenues. Consumer Affairs capability for handling such increased oversight was substantially diminished by budget actions in 1975 and 1976 which reduced staff from a total of 8 to 5 persons. Failure to provide the increased monitoring could jeopardize supervision and evaluation of Arlington cable television.While the primary assignment the new position would be to cable television, when time and workload permit, the incumbent would also assist in other Consumer Affairs activities.

PERSONNEL (MAN YEARS) SERVICE CLASSIFICATION	FY 78 RECOMM	FY 78 ALT 1	FY 78 CHANGE
Executive Director	.12	.12	.0
Services Clerk			
Administrative Aide	.00	1.00	1.0
TOTAL			
TEMPORARY FUNDS (DOLLARS)			

FISCAL SUMMARY	FY 78 RECOMM	FY 78 ALT 1	FY 78 (CHANGE +/-)
COST			
PERSONNEL	4,642	19,141	14,499
NON-PERSONNEL	355	355	-0-
TOTAL	4,997	19,496	14,499
REVENUE			
FEES			
GRANTS & OTHER			
TOTAL			
NET GENERAL FUND SUPPORT	4,997	19,496	14,499
% CHANGE FROM FY 78 RECOMMENDED ACTIVITY BUDGET			290 %

C U R R E N T

CURRENT ACTIVITY DESCRIPTION WEIGHTS AND MEASURES PURPOSE & OBJECTIVES: The purpose of this activity is to ensure that citizens receive accurate weight and measure of their purchases through the enforcement of applicable state laws and federal regulations and standards. Specific tasks are to check and seal each gasoline pump at least twice annually, to check-weigh pre-packaged goods at each grocery at least once annually and to check and seal scales at least twice a year. In addition, special investigations are conducted when there are suspected violations.

PERFORMANCE MEASURES	FY 75	FY 76	FIRST HALF OF FY 77
Stores visited, scales	231	167	88
Scales inspected	784	776	358
Gas stations inspected	196	185	43
Gas pumps tested	1,245	1,278	348
Packages check-weighed	87,709	84,341	15,362

PERSONNEL (MAN YEARS) SERVICE CLASSIFICATION	FY 76 ACTUAL	FY 77 BUDGET	FY 78 RECOMM	FY 78 CHANGE
Executive Director	.04	.03	.04	
Weights & Measures Inspector	.60	.60	.60	
TOTAL	.64	.63	.64	
TEMPORARY FUNDS (DOLLARS)	90	90		

FISCAL SUMMARY	FY 76 ACTUAL	FY 77 BUDGET	FY 78 RECOMM
COST			
PERSONNEL	15,030	11,638	9,577
NON-PERSONNEL	1,180	1,520	1,560
TOTAL	16,210	13,158	11,137
REVENUE			
FEES			
GRANTS & OTHER			
TOTAL			
NET GENERAL FUND SUPPORT	16,210	13,158	11,137
% OF DEPARTMENTAL LOCAL BUDGET	14 %	12 %	10 %
% CHANGE FROM FY 77			(15) %

R E D U C T I O N

ALTERNATIVE 1 DESCRIBE CHANGE, IMPACT AND CONSEQUENCES This alternative eliminates the Weights and Measures Inspector position and Arlington's direct participation in enforcement of weights and measures laws and regulations. Arlington is not required by law to perform these inspections. If the position were eliminated, we would request the state to assume full responsibility for the function in Arlington. It is uncertain what level of service the state would be able to provide, but it would no doubt be at a level considerably less than Arlington has been providing. The elimination of the position would also decrease the level of general consumer services, since the Weights and Measures Inspector has devoted 60% of his time to weights and measures inspections and 40% to general consumer services including responding to citizens' complaints. Besides the elimination of the weights and measures program, this alternative would result in a 10% reduction in man-years assigned to the Consumer Affairs activity of this office.

PERSONNEL (MAN YEARS) SERVICE CLASSIFICATION	FY 78 RECOMM	FY 78 ALT 2	FY 78 CHANGE
Weights & Measures Inspector	1.0*	-0-	(1.0)
TOTAL	1.0	-0-	(1.0)
TEMPORARY FUNDS (DOLLARS)			

FISCAL SUMMARY	FY 78 RECOMM	FY 78 ALT 2	FY 78 (CHANGE +/-)
COST			
PERSONNEL	13,976	-0-	(13,976)
NON-PERSONNEL	1,200	-0-	(1,200)
TOTAL	15,176*	-0-	(15,176)
REVENUE			
FEES			
GRANTS & OTHER			
TOTAL			
NET GENERAL FUND SUPPORT	15,176	-0-	(15,176)
% CHANGE FROM FY 78 RECOMMENDED ACTIVITY BUDGET			(100) %

* Full cost of inspector position and supportive services included.

Exhibit C-5
Arlington County Budget: Police Department Organization Chart, FY 1978

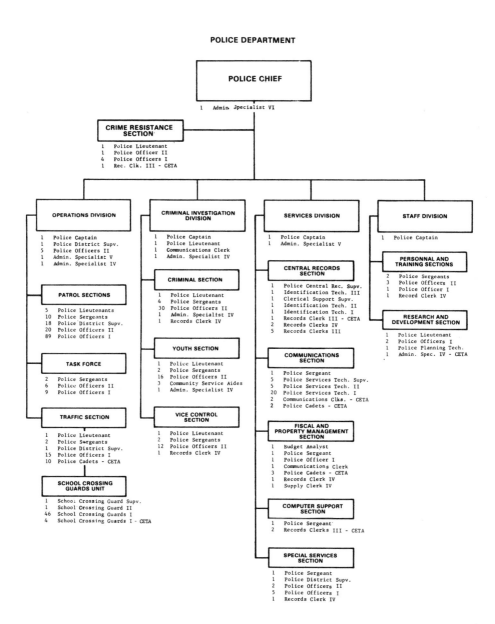

Exhibit C-6
Arlington County Budget: Police Department Summary, FY 1978

PAGE	ACTIVITY DESCRIPTION	FISCAL YEAR 1977 APPROVED PROGRAM LEVEL			RECOMMENDED PROGRAM LEVEL			FISCAL YEAR 1978 FUNDING OPTIONS REDUCED PROGRAM LEVEL			INCREASED PROGRAM LEVEL		
		Costs	Revenues	Net General Fund	Costs	Revenues	Net General Fund	Costs	Revenues	Net General Fund	Costs	Revenues	Net General Fund
	POLICE DEPARTMENT												
	ADMINISTRATION	2,405,822	48,059	2,357,763	2,650,457	55,880	2,594,577				19,240		19,240
106	– Eliminate Holiday Pay							(140,000)		(140,000)			
106	– Eliminate Court Pay							(48,000)		(48,000)			
106													
	CRIME PREVENTION	1,344,091	2,066	1,342,025	1,562,529	2,389	1,560,140						
107	– Reduce Youth Resources Activities							(66,038)		(66,038)			
107	– Fund Summer Camp Operating Expenses												
107													
	TRAFFIC CONTROL	978,744	101,590	877,154	1,130,231	120,244	1,009,987						
108	– Reduce Traffic Patrol							(58,879)		(58,879)			
108	– Reduce accident Investigation							(91,039)		(91,039)			
108	– Reduce Enforcement of Non-Hazardous Violations							(30,444)		(30,444)			
109	– Eliminate Nine School Crossing Guards							(50,538)		(50,538)			
109	– Transfer Crossing Guards to Community Activities Budget							(176,716)		(176,716)			
109													
	CRIME REDUCTION, INVESTIGATION AND APPREHENSION	1,920,435	4,042	1,916,393	2,229,977	4,778	2,225,199						
110	– Reduce Investigations of Crimes Against Property							(101,436)		(101,436)			
110	– Reduce Vice Investigations							(28,304)		(28,304)			
111	– Reduce Involvement in minor Criminal Cases							(14,310)		(14,310)			
	MAINTENANCE OF PUBLIC ORDER	159,052	270	158,782	172,409	265	172,144						
111	– Reduce Emergency Response Capability							(92,517)		(92,517)			
111													
	PUBLIC AND EMERGENCY SERVICES	506,991	41,260	465,731	522,064	51,340	470,724						
112	– Reduce Missing Persons Investigations							(18,576)		(18,576)			
112													
	TECHNICAL SERVICES	1,256,025	44,321	1,201,704	1,038,401	61,993	976,408						
112	– Consolidate Police-Fire Communications							(67,260)		(67,260)			
113													
	INSPECTIONAL SERVICES	85,607		85,607	125,970		125,970						
113	– Reduce Inspectional Services							(16,000)		(16,000)			
113													
	TOTAL	8,656,767	251,608	8,405,159	9,432,038	296,889	9,135,149	(1,000,057)		(1,000,057)	19,240		19,240

Exhibit C-7

Arlington County Budget: Nondepartmental Summary, FY 1978

PAGE	ACTIVITY DESCRIPTION	FISCAL YEAR 1977 APPROVED PROGRAM LEVEL			FISCAL YEAR 1978 FUNDING OPTIONS								
					RECOMMENDED PROGRAM LEVEL			REDUCED PROGRAM LEVEL			INCREASED PROGRAM LEVEL		
		Costs	Revenues	Net General Fund	Costs	Revenues	Net General Fund	Costs	Revenues	Net General Fund	Costs	Revenues	Net General Fund
	NON-DEPARTMENTAL												
219	EMPLOYEE BENEFITS	350,050		350,050	520,000		520,000						
220 220	INSURANCE - Self-insure Major Insurance Coverages	513,000		513,000	555,000		555,000	(42,000)		(42,000)			
221	OTHER	1,554,334		1,554,334	2,833,100		2,833,100						
	TOTAL	2,417,384		2,417,384	3,908,100		3,908,100	(42,000)		(42,000)			

Exhibit C-8
Arlington County Budget: Nondepartmental, FY 1978

CURRENT ACTIVITY DESCRIPTION INSURANCE

PURPOSE & OBJECTIVES Arlington County's insurance program is a combination of purchased insurance coverage, self insured plans (separate appropriation to pay claims) and self-assumed risks (no separate appropriation). The major insurance policies purchased by the county are Comprehensive General Liability, Automotive Liability, and Fire and Allied Perils. The county had purchased excess Worker's Compensation coverage, but the policy was cancelled effective January 1, 1977.

The county self insures Worker's Compensation for both the county and the schools, and self-assumes the payment of certain losses which are not covered by the insurance policies.

ALTERNATIVE 1. DESCRIBE CHANGE IMPACT AND CONSEQUENCES The cost of insurance premiums is increasing much faster than the county's losses would indicate that it should, making the purchase of insurance coverage less cost effective. One alternative to paying increased insurance costs is to self-insure all major lines of insurance coverage. The following is a breakdown of the Fiscal 1978 estimated costs of the self-insurance program:

Consultants		$ 1,000
Insurance Premiums		24,000
Faithful Performance Bond	2,500	
Excess Fire and Allied Perils	20,000	
Volunteer Fire and Auxiliary Police	1,500	
Accidental Injury Policy		
Additional Staff		21,000
Subtotal		$ 46,000

Estimated Claim Payment		$ 250,000
Worker's Compensation		50,000
Auto Liability		
General Liability		15,000
Administration of Claims (Supplemental Legal, Adjustment & Computer Services)		29,000
Subtotal		$ 344,000

First Year Costs	$ 390,000
Reserve Fund	123,000
Total Costs	$ 513,000

The self-insurance program as outlined above would provide a full time position to handle most property damage claims and to coordinate a county-wide safety effort. Accident, safety and claims records would be maintained by the half-time clerical position. A trust fund should be established to cover the payment of routine claims and as a guarantee that an unanticipated catastrophic loss could be covered without a special appropriation from the general fund. So that a reserve of substantial size can be established within five years, a $123,000 appropriation is recommended for this purpose. This would maintain the insurance program at the Fiscal 1977 approved level, which is $42,000 less than the current insurance program would cost in Fiscal 1976.

PERSONNEL (MAN YEARS) SERVICE CLASSIFICATION	FY 76 ACTUAL	FY 77 BUDGET	FY 78 RECOMM
TOTAL			
TEMPORARY FUNDS (DOLLARS)			

FISCAL SUMMARY	FY 76 ACTUAL	FY 77 BUDGET	FY 78 RECOMM
COST			
PERSONNEL	-0-	-0-	-0-
NON-PERSONNEL	451,230	513,000	555,000
TOTAL	451,230	513,000	555,000
REVENUE			
FEES			
GRANTS & OTHER			
TOTAL			
NET GENERAL FUND SUPPORT	451,230	513,000	555,000
% CHANGE FROM FY 77			8 %
% OF DEPARTMENTAL LOCAL BUDGET	42 %	21 %	14 %

PERSONNEL (MAN YEARS) SERVICE CLASSIFICATION	FY 78 RECOMM	FY 78 ALT 1	FY 78 CHANGE
Administrative Aide	-0-	1.0	1.0
Administrative Specialist IV	-0-	.5	.5
TOTAL	-0-	1.5	1.5
TEMPORARY FUNDS (DOLLARS)			

FISCAL SUMMARY	FY 78 RECOMM	FY 78 ALT 1	FY 78 CHANGE +/-
COST			
PERSONNEL	-0-	21,000	21,000
NON-PERSONNEL	555,000	492,000	(63,000)
TOTAL	555,000	513,000	(42,000)
REVENUE			
FEES			
GRANTS & OTHER			
TOTAL			
NET GENERAL FUND SUPPORT	555,000	513,000	(42,000)
% CHANGE FROM FY 78 RECOMMENDED ACTIVITY BUDGET			(8) %

232

Exhibit C-9
Arlington County Budget: Social Services Organization Chart, FY 1978

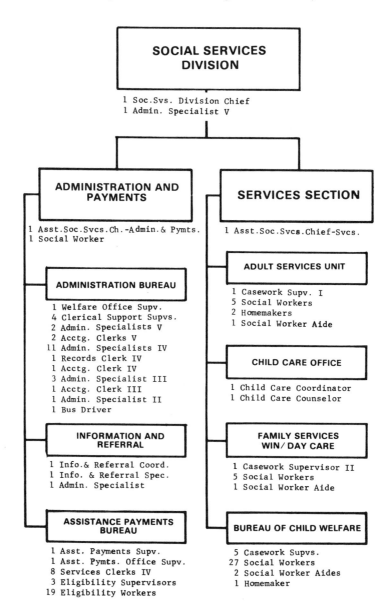

Exhibit C-10
Arlington County Budget: Social Services Summary, FY 1978

PAGE	ACTIVITY DESCRIPTION	FISCAL YEAR 1977 APPROVED PROGRAM LEVEL			FISCAL YEAR 1978 FUNDING OPTIONS RECOMMENDED PROGRAM LEVEL			REDUCED PROGRAM LEVEL			INCREASED PROGRAM LEVEL		
		Costs	Revenues	Net General Fund	Costs	Revenues	Net General Fund	Costs	Revenues	Net General Fund	Costs	Revenues	Net General Fund
	DEPARTMENT OF HUMAN RESOURCES												
	DIVISION OF SOCIAL SERVICES												
233	SOCIAL SERVICES ADMINISTRATION - Add Consultant Funds	603,844	458,228	145,616	466,975	347,099	119,876				10,000	7,500	2,500
233	SERVICES INTAKE	203,305	151,661	51,644	211,207	155,532	55,675						
234	INFORMATION AND REFERRAL	103,560	81,017	22,543	107,005	83,938	23,067						
234	CHILD CARE OFFICE	66,672	49,959	16,713	64,423	47,390	17,033						
235	ADULT AND GERIATRIC SERVICES - Add one Social worker Position	517,143	396,557	120,586	486,921	365,241	121,680				17,923	14,258	3,665
236	FAMILY SERVICES - Add one Family Service Worker	707,992	580,607	127,385	710,775	539,319	171,456				19,107	14,330	4,777
237	CHILD PLACEMENT - Eliminate Casework Supervisor Position	1,193,385	807,295	386,100	1,580,903	1,129,071	451,832	(24,976)	(16,835)	(8,141)			
239	PREVENTIVE/PROTECTIVE SERVICES - Add two former Pro-Child Grant Positions	329,021	259,403	69,319	201,194	148,069	53,125				31,560	23,314	8,246
240 242 242 242 243	ASSISTANCE PAYMENTS - Add two Eligibility Workers - Reduce Aid to Dependent Children - Reduce General Relief - Increase State-Local Hospitalization	5,264,656	4,400,136	1,864,520	3,260,996	1,642,102	1,618,894	(98,468) (65,177)	(13,218) (40,448)	(85,250) (24,729)	29,438 270,300	19,816 91,121	10,022 179,179
	TOTAL	9,689,578	7,154,052	2,540,625	7,706,391	4,457,411	3,439,558	(188,621)	(70,501)	(119,120)	378,648	170,179	208,289

Exhibit C-11

Arlington County Budget: Proposed Social Services Increase, FY 1978

ALTERNATIVE 4 DESCRIBE CHANGE, IMPACT AND CONSEQUENCES The funding of the State-Local Hospitalization (SLH) program would be increased under this alternative. The recommended continuing budget for Fiscal 1978 contains $383,000 for SLH, which is the funding level for Fiscal 1977. The additional local cost of $179,000 shown at the right is the estimated requirement for the following:

a) An estimated $97,000 in local funds is required to continue the program according to existing policies. The increase will allow for increases in contract rates based on Fiscal 1977 cost information for hospitals. Also, the increase will allow for the continuation of the present policy of placing no limits on days of care, except in cases involving alcoholic or psychiatric admissions.

b) An additional $82,000 will be required to pay for costs incurred by persons who are eligible for Medicaid but have exceeded the twenty-one day limit allowed by the State Health Department.

PERSONNEL (MAN-YEARS) SERVICE CLASSIFICATION	FY 78 RECOMM	FY 78 ALT 1	FY 78 CHANGE		FISCAL SUMMARY	FY 78 RECOMM	FY 78 ALT 1	FY 78 (CHANGE +/-)
					COST			
					PERSONNEL	548,441	548,441	
					NON-PERSONNEL	2,709,680	2,979,980	270,300
					TOTAL	3,258,121	3,528,621	270,300
					REVENUE			
					FEES			
					GRANTS & OTHER	1,642,192	1,733,313	91,121
					TOTAL	1,642,192	1,733,313	91,121
					NET GENERAL FUND SUPPORT	1,615,929	1,795,108	179,179
TOTAL					% CHANGE FROM FY 78 RECOMMENDED ACTIVITY BUDGET			11 %
TEMPORARY FUNDS (DOLLARS)								

ALTERNATIVE _____ DESCRIBE CHANGE, IMPACT AND CONSEQUENCES

PERSONNEL (MAN-YEARS) SERVICE CLASSIFICATION	FY 78 RECOMM	FY 78 ALT 1	FY 78 CHANGE		FISCAL SUMMARY	FY 78 RECOMM	FY 78 ALT 1	FY 78 (CHANGE +/-)
					COST			
					PERSONNEL			
					NON-PERSONNEL			
					TOTAL			
					REVENUE			
					FEES			
					GRANTS & OTHER			
					TOTAL			
					NET GENERAL FUND SUPPORT			
TOTAL					% CHANGE FROM FY 78 RECOMMENDED ACTIVITY BUDGET			%
TEMPORARY FUNDS (DOLLARS)								

ALTERNATIVE _____ DESCRIBE CHANGE, IMPACT AND CONSEQUENCES

PERSONNEL (MAN-YEARS) SERVICE CLASSIFICATION	FY 78 RECOMM	FY 78 ALT 2	FY 78 CHANGE		FISCAL SUMMARY	FY 78 RECOMM	FY 78 ALT 2	FY 78 (CHANGE +/-)
					COST			
					PERSONNEL			
					NON-PERSONNEL			
					TOTAL			
					REVENUE			
					FEES			
					GRANTS & OTHER			
					TOTAL			
					NET GENERAL FUND SUPPORT			
TOTAL					% CHANGE FROM FY 78 RECOMMENDED ACTIVITY BUDGET			%
TEMPORARY FUNDS (DOLLARS)								

Index

About the Author

Joseph S. Wholey has been a member of the Washington Metropolitan Area Transit Authority Board of Directors since 1976, a member of the County Board of Arlington, Virginia, since 1971, and senior research-staff member at the Urban Institute since 1968. A graduate of Catholic University and Harvard University, Dr. Wholey's major professional work has been in program evaluation, both at the Urban Institute and in the Office of Secretary of Health, Education and Welfare, where he served as Director of Program Evaluation.

Dr. Wholey is the author of *Federal Evaluation Policy* and many journal articles and reports on program evaluation and public policy.